NOT THE CHILCOT REPORT

PETER OBORNE is associate editor of the *Spectator* and a former chief political commentator of the *Daily Telegraph*. He writes a column for the *Daily Mail* and for *Middle East Eye*. His books include *The Rise of Political Lying*; *The Triumph of the Political Class*; *A Dangerous Delusion: Why the West is Wrong About Nuclear Iran* (written with David Morrison); and *Wounded Tiger: A History of Cricket in Pakistan*.

NOT THE CHILCOT REPORT

PETER OBORNE

First published in the UK in 2016 by Head of Zeus Ltd

9 7 5 3 1 2 4 6 8

A catalogue record for this book is available from
the British Library.

ISBN (HB): 9781784977962
ISBN (E): 9781784977955

Typeset by Adrian McLaughlin

Printed in the UK by Clays Ltd, St Ives Plc

Head of Zeus Ltd
Clerkenwell House
45–47 Clerkenwell Green
London ECIR OHT

WWW.HEADOFZEUS.COM

CONTENTS

FOREWORD

I started to ponder this book when repeated delays and obstructions meant that it had become doubtful whether Sir John Chilcot's report would ever appear in a worthwhile form.

I reflected that almost all the relevant testimony could already be found on the excellent Iraq Inquiry website. I concluded that it was possible for an interested observer to study the evidence presented to Sir John Chilcot, follow leads of his own, then reach his or her own conclusions.

I have asked four key questions: Did Tony Blair lie to the British people ahead of the war? Was the war lawful? Did Tony Blair and George W. Bush reach a secret agreement when they met at Crawford in 2002? Has the Iraq War left Britain a safer place, as was promised? I have also tried to narrate the background to the invasion of Iraq, and to spell out some of the consequences, and the lessons that should be learned.

Above all I hope this book will assist lay readers who want to make sense of the Chilcot Report. It is anticipated that Sir John's report will stretch to around 2 million words (nearly four times the length of *War and Peace*), while dozens of those involved will be criticized, suggesting an unfocused, scattergun approach. Making sense of this mass of detail will be very hard. I have tried to focus on the most important issues, and assemble the essential evidence.

The most complex and controversial dilemma I faced concerned the moral character of Tony Blair. Did he lie to Parliament and the British people to make the case for war? Some good judges, including the chief weapons inspector Hans Blix, a former diplomat, have told me that they judged he did.[1]

A lie contains two separate elements. It may well embrace a falsehood, but above all it must be uttered in the knowledge that it is false. A lie does not mean only pure invention. It also embraces presenting assertion and speculation as certain, corroborated fact. It must be intended to deceive.

Tony Blair has consistently asserted that he did not lie in the run-up to the invasion of Iraq. He agrees that he might have made mistakes, and even accepted that some of his statements about Saddam's weapons of mass destruction were wrong. However, he has been adamant that, whatever the faults of others, he himself acted in good faith.

Here is one recent example of this self-justification. Last October, during an interview with CNN, Mr Blair told Fareed Zakaria: 'I apologize for the fact that the intelligence we received was wrong ...'.[2] Here Mr Blair is placing the blame on the British

---

1   *Peter Oborne's Chilcot Report*, Radio 4, 29 October 2015.

2   http://edition.cnn.com/2015/10/25/europe/tony-blair-iraq-war/ The full quote reads as follows: 'I can say that I apologize for the fact that the intelligence we received was wrong because, even though he [Saddam Hussein] had used

intelligence services for producing erroneous information, which he as prime minister innocently passed on to the British public.

I investigated this account. It does not stand up to scrutiny. I demolish the idea that Tony Blair simply reiterated what he was told by the intelligence services. In fact he exaggerated and misrepresented the intelligence he was receiving from the Joint Intelligence Committee.

Lord Butler, who in 2004 carried out the review into the use of intelligence in the lead-up to the Iraq invasion, has since been damning about this:

> ... neither the United Kingdom nor the United States had the intelligence that proved conclusively that Iraq had those weapons [weapons of mass destruction]. The Prime Minister was disingenuous about that. The United Kingdom intelligence community told him on 23 August 2002 that, 'we ... know little about Iraq's chemical and biological weapons work since late 1988'. The Prime Minister did not tell us that. Indeed, he told Parliament only just over a month later that the picture painted by our intelligence services was 'extensive, detailed and authoritative'. Those words could simply not have been justified by the material that the intelligence community provided to him.[3]

---

chemical weapons extensively against his own people, against others, the programme in the form that we thought it was did not exist in the way that we thought.'

3   Lords *Hansard*, 22 February 2007, Col 1231. These remarks were stronger and less measured than those contained in Lord Butler's original report. As time passed, Lord Butler may have felt able to speak more freely.

So Tony Blair made false statements about Saddam Hussein's so-called weapons of mass destruction even though he had access to intelligence reports that proved that what he was saying was wrong. There can moreover be no doubt that Mr Blair read the underlying intelligence, because Mr Blair himself revealed as much in his evidence to the Chilcot Inquiry.[4]

Does this make Tony Blair a liar? It is still just about arguable that it does not. Remember: a lie must be uttered with intent to deceive. Otherwise it is not a lie. Mr Blair and his supporters can continue to say that he believed what he was saying about Saddam's weapons of mass destruction to be true. Ultimately nobody can challenge this – unless Mr Blair were on record as admitting that he knew at the time he uttered it that what he was saying was false. He has made no such statement.

So is Mr Blair in the clear? Not at all. Back in 2003 Mr Blair was British prime minister. His remarks concerning British intelligence were used to justify a war in which countless people were to die, including 179 British servicemen. It is surely axiomatic that, if a British prime minister cites the intelligence services, the British public and Parliament are entitled to assume that he is telling the truth.

Furthermore, there is a discernible pattern to the way Mr Blair and his circle dealt with the British people ahead of the war. They highlighted information that placed the threat posed by the Iraqi dictator in the worst possible light. They kept quiet meanwhile about relevant facts that damaged their cause.

---

4   See his Statement to the Iraq Inquiry, 14 January 2011.

They misrepresented the actions and motives of those opposed to war. Some of Mr Blair's wildest statements about WMD were made to Parliament. This meant that he repeatedly flouted his own ministerial code of conduct, which insisted that 'it is of paramount importance that Ministers give accurate and truthful information to Parliament, correcting any inadvertent error at the earliest opportunity'.

There was never any attempt to correct false statements after they had been uttered. In fact Tony Blair's claim that the intelligence picture was 'extensive, detailed and authoritative', dismantled by Lord Butler above, remains on the parliamentary record some *thirteen years* after it was made.[5] So do other false statements.[6]

All that said, the fact remains that no outside observer can say what was going on inside the mind of Tony Blair as war loomed in 2003. The former prime minister's claim that he acted in good faith may therefore be ultimately impossible to refute.

Accepting that Mr Blair acted in good faith, however, brings with it a fresh series of problems. Mr Blair admits that he read the intelligence provided for him by the JIC. Why did he repeatedly

---

5   *Hansard*, House of Commons Debates, 24 September 2002, Col 3.
6   For example this statement concerning the second 'dodgy' dossier to the House of Commons: 'We issued further intelligence over the weekend about the infrastructure of concealment [in Iraq]. It is obviously difficult when we publish intelligence reports, but I hope that people have some sense of the integrity of our security services. They are not publishing this, or giving us this information, and making it up. It is the intelligence that they are receiving, and we are passing it on to people.' In fact this document had not been seen in advance by British intelligence, let alone published by it. This statement remains on the parliamentary record to this day. *Hansard*, House of Commons Debates, 3 February 2005, Col 25.

pass on to the British people such a misleading account of the intelligence he was receiving? Why did he give a selective and therefore false account of the report by the United Nations weapons inspectors in his speech to Parliament on 18 March 2003? Why did he give such a selective account of the French President Jacques Chirac's position on a second resolution in that 18 March speech? Similar questions abound.

In order to claim that he was acting in good faith, defenders of Mr Blair have no choice but to concede that he also took leave of reality. Those who want to claim that Mr Blair did not lie are therefore forced to enter the realm of psychology rather than politics and claim that he was living in some parallel universe.

On the face of things this would seem absurd. Mr Blair was surrounded by capable people. These included private secretaries, intelligence chiefs, cabinet ministers, press handlers. It was their job to ensure that the prime minister kept his feet on the ground.

Here at last Mr Blair's supporters can point to a notable point in their favour. It is not obvious that the prime minister's high-powered counsellors did keep his feet on the ground. I have found no evidence that David Manning, foreign policy adviser inside Downing Street as war loomed, ever tried to correct Tony Blair. Neither have I found protests from Foreign Secretary Jack Straw. Nor from Jonathan Powell, Downing Street chief of staff. Nor Alastair Campbell, Director of Communications.

More importantly still, I have not discovered any alarm from either the Joint Intelligence Committee or the Secret Intelligence Service that the prime minister was misrepresenting their intelligence. This failure to challenge Mr Blair means that the Secret

Intelligence Service in effect colluded with the prime minister as he led Britain into this calamitous war. (I show that MI5, the domestic intelligence service, emerges much more creditably.)

All this means that we are entitled to assert without contradiction that the Blair government led Britain into war on the back of a series of lies about the threat posed by Saddam Hussein. And what of Mr Blair himself? He was the head of that government. He was never backward in claiming credit for the successes of his administration. He must also take personal responsibility for the moral errors of his administration. That is why, after a great deal of thought, I have concluded that Mr Blair can reasonably be accused of lying to take Britain to war.

It has been a chastening experience researching and writing this book. As I studied the events leading up to the war, I felt a growing sense of dismay and ultimately shame and remorse at my own performance as political columnist for *The Spectator*.

This was because I realized it was perfectly possible for an assiduous journalist *at the time* to have uncovered many of the lies and falsehoods being uttered by politicians and officials.

I failed to do so. It is no excuse that I was part of a wider failure. Though there were shining exceptions, the mainstream media as a whole failed to tell truth to power in the run-up to the invasion of Iraq.[7] It should always be taken into account that it was not only politicians and officials who failed in their duty.

---

7   I dealt with this subject in Chapter 12 (entitled 'The Media Class and the Iraq War') of my book, *The Triumph of the Political Class*, Simon & Schuster, 2007, pp. 271–93.

This was not true of my friend Dr David Morrison. He was right at the time and since has written a series of brilliant papers on the subject of the Iraq War. Large parts of the book – in particular Chapters 5, 6, 8, 9 and 10 – are closely based on Dr Morrison's work.[8]

Our original intention was to write this book together. Unfortunately, David and I found our interpretation of certain issues – in particular the long background to the invasion – made this plan impossible, and so I have ended up authoring it on my own. However, it does draw very heavily on his original and path-breaking analysis and contains sections of his clear-headed writing. This book would have been quite impossible without Dr Morrison.

The second debt is to my long-term collaborator Richard Heller. Mr Heller has drafted long sections of this work, including most of the narrative sections concerning the run-up to war and its aftermath. He has always been a huge pleasure to deal with. Mr Heller, once an adviser to the Labour statesman Denis Healey, has a profound understanding of the Iraq War and the Labour Party, and this book could not have been written without him.

In common with many others, I owe a huge debt to Chris Ames, the scrupulous and indefatigable investigative journalist who for many years has wrestled with the bodyguard of falsehood and mystery surrounding Britain's role in the Iraq War. Chris is

---

8   See in particular *Iraq: lies, half-truths and omissions*, November 2003 and
     Iraq: How regime change was dressed up as disarmament, December 2005
     (at www.david-morrison.org.uk) and openDemocracy articles: *Lies, half-*
     truths and omissions on the road to war against Iraq; *Al-Qaeda, ISIS, and*
     the wider fallout from the Iraq invasion; *Did Blair secretly promise Bush*
     regime change in Iraq?; *Was Britain's military action in Iraq legal?* (at www.
     opendemocracy.net/author/david-morrison).

editor of the online Iraq Inquiry Digest (www.iraqinquirydigest. com) which has not only tracked the daily progress (to use the term loosely) of the inquiry but also revealed new information and allowed the public a means of commenting on the inquiry and influencing its agenda. I am grateful to him for sharing his own copious knowledge and for reading this book. In addition I am grateful to Peter Jenkins, Henry Foy and Shashank Joshi for casting their expert eyes over it. Richard Sanders, producer of *Afghanistan: The Lion's Last Roar?* for BBC Two has helped me understand the wider context of Britain's war in Afghanistan.

I can't express my gratitude to Dr Tom Roberts too highly. Tom has been heavily involved in drafting, fact checking and assisting the book at a late stage. He has lifted a huge burden from my shoulders. Of course all remaining errors of fact and judgement are my own responsibility.

I am also very grateful to Innes Bowen for commissioning *Peter Oborne's Chilcot Report* for BBC Radio 4 last autumn. I was able to develop the analysis and interview significant figures. Hannah Barnes, who produced the programme, helped me form many of my judgements. Lindsay Codsi has provided, as always, invaluable administrative assistance. I would like to thank Thomas Hatherley for his work on the proofs. Also thanks to my publisher, Neil Belton, agent, Andrew Gordon and the team at Head of Zeus, including Georgina Blackwell and Clémence Jacquinet who have had to put up with a great deal, as has Martin Soames, our superb lawyer. And finally my wife Martine and family, for allowing me to vanish for long periods to write and think.

LONDON, 18 APRIL 2016

ABBREVIATIONS
AND ACRONYMS

AQ	al-Qaeda
BW	biological weapons
CB	chemical or biological
CENTCOM	(US) Central Command
CIA	Central Intelligence Agency
CND	Campaign for Nuclear Disarmament
CPA	Coalition Provisional Administration
CW	chemical weapons
FAC	Foreign Affairs Committee (House of Commons)
FCO	Foreign & Commonwealth Office
IAEA	International Atomic Energy Agency
ICC	International Criminal Court
ICJ	International Court of Justice
IED	improvised explosive device
IS	Islamic State
ISC	Intelligence and Security Committee

ISIS	Islamic State of Iraq and al-Sham
JIC	Joint Intelligence Committee
MoD	Ministry of Defence
NATO	North Atlantic Treaty Organization
OHRA	Office for Humanitarian and Reconstruction Assistance
OP	Operative Paragraph
OPEC	Organization of the Petroleum Exporting Countries
PLO	Palestine Liberation Organization
PRT	provisional reconstruction team
SAS	Special Air Service
SCR	Security Council resolution
SIS	Secret Intelligence Service
UN	United Nations
UNMOVIC	United Nations Monitoring, Verification and Inspection Commission
UNSC	United Nations Security Council
UNSCR	United Nations Security Council Resolution
UNSCOM	United Nations Special Commission
WDD	weapons of daily destruction
WMD	weapons of mass destruction

ONE

IRAQ: THE DEFINING CALAMITY OF THE POST-COLD WAR ERA

'We were with you at the first,
we will stay with you to the last.'

Tony Blair[1]

On 1 May 2003 President George W. Bush announced the end of major combat operations in Iraq, posing in flying gear on an aircraft carrier beneath a banner stating 'Mission Accomplished'.

In fairness to Bush, he was not responsible for the banner. But the image would haunt him, as it became obvious to the American people that his Iraq mission was not accomplished and never would be.

---

1   Tony Blair, speaking at the Labour Party conference in October 2001, shortly after 9/11. The 'you' being Americans.

The Iraq War failed in both its immediate and its strategic objectives. Its promoters had depicted Saddam Hussein as a threat to the United States and to the international world order.

In fact, Saddam's regime was little threat to any other country, was far from acquiring serious weapons of mass destruction (WMD) capacity, and was never remotely likely to supply such weapons to al-Qaeda or any other terrorist group. Al-Qaeda had no support from Saddam and no base in Saddam-controlled Iraq. His fall, however, allowed them to establish themselves in Iraq. They did not acquire WMD, because there were none to acquire, but they did acquire thousands of WDD – weapons of daily destruction – which cost thousands of lives, mostly Iraqi, but also American and British.

The Iraq War was part of an ambitious 'forward' policy in which the United States would use its power unilaterally to achieve American goals in the Middle East and throughout the world. Saddam Hussein would be replaced by a pro-American, pro-free market democracy (in a key oil producer with a major influence on the price of oil). This new Iraq would project Western values, counter the threat of Iran and underpin a new and stable order in the Middle East.

Instead, the fall of Saddam Hussein led to a long period of violent disorder. This in turn brought about the near-destruction of the Iraqi state, which escalated into a sectarian war between the country's Shia majority and a Sunni minority which felt dispossessed following the fall of Saddam. Iran, meanwhile, acquired new influence within Iraq and throughout the Middle East. Far from embracing Western values, parts of Iraq fell into the hands of terrorist groups who were even more fanatical than al-Qaeda.

Only one cause united militant Sunni and Shia opponents: a common hostility to the foreign occupier. British troops, never given the means to achieve their tasks as an occupying power, became onlookers in southern Iraq. In the summer of 2009 the majority were withdrawn, along with American combat troops, but several thousand allied troops remained as trainers and support for the Iraqi army until the final withdrawal in 2011. By that time, Britain had lost 179 soldiers in Iraq, the Americans over 4,000.[2] Thousands more suffered permanent physical or psychological damage. The number of Iraqi casualties is beyond computation.[3]

---

2   See www.icasualties.org.

3   As it turned out, the numbers killed in Iraq during the invasion and since have been horrendous, though the precise number will never be known. 'We don't do body counts,' General Tommy Franks, the US commander of the invading forces, famously remarked. If the bodies are Iraqi, he should have added. The bodies of the invading forces were counted precisely – 4,845 were killed (US 4,495, UK 179 and others 141). See http://icasualties.org/IRAQ/index.aspx.

One source that is often quoted for civilian deaths is the Iraq Body Count organization. Since 2003, they have made an admirable attempt to document civilian deaths in Iraq. But they register only the numbers of civilians killed that are reported in respected English-language media and then only if a fatal incident is reported by at least two independent sources. If the data from the two sources differ, the larger number is regarded as the 'maximum', the smaller one as the 'minimum'. At the time of writing (4 April 2016), the Iraq Body Count 'minimum' figure is 156,316 and the 'maximum' is 174,838. See https://www.iraqbodycount.org.

This is a reliable count of the number of Iraqi civilians that we can be sure have been killed since March 2003. However, since it doesn't register casualties that are not reported by two independent sources in English-language media, it merely sets a lower limit on the actual number of civilian deaths. Other researchers have sought to estimate the actual number of civilian deaths. For example, in October 2006, the British medical journal *The Lancet* published a study by the Bloomberg School of Public Health at Johns Hopkins University. This was based on a poll of a representative

The war had some other unintended consequences. The neo-conservatives – among whom the most eminent in the Bush administration were Vice-President Dick Cheney, Defense Secretary Donald Rumsfeld and his deputy Paul Wolfowitz – had sought to establish a doctrine of preventative self-defence whereby the United States would act against perceived threats on the basis of intelligence data. Instead the Iraq War gave the American people a strong aversion to preventative war and indeed any foreign intervention which involved the use of ground troops. Today, the United States and Britain prefer instead to intervene by means of air power, as in Libya, or unmanned drones, as against the Taliban in Afghanistan and Pakistan. These are forms of warfare which inevitably kill innocent people, whose gains are always likely to be temporary and which give the Western powers no means of controlling events on the ground in the countries concerned. The Iraq War also discredited the intelligence services in both countries and made it harder, if not impossible, for future leaders to take their people into an intelligence-led war.

Notwithstanding its terrible aftermath, George W. Bush and Tony Blair – the two leaders who had ordered the invasion – continue to justify their decision on the basis that it dislodged

---

selection of 1,850 households and almost 13,000 participants, compiling deaths in Iraq both in the fifteen months before the war and in the forty months after. By this means, the study estimated the war and its aftermath had resulted in an additional 655,000 deaths by July 2006. See 'Mortality After the 2003 Invasion of Iraq: A Cross-Sectional Cluster Sample Survey', Burnham, Gilbert et al., *The Lancet*, Vol. 368, Issue 9545, pp. 1421–8.

Physicians for Social Responsibility published a review of the various estimates in March 2015. They concluded on the basis of this study and other later ones that 'the war has, directly or indirectly, killed around 1 million people in Iraq'. See http://www.psr.org/assets/pdfs/body-count.pdf.

Saddam Hussein, the bloodthirsty dictator of Iraq, and removed a serious threat to their nations and all the Western states.

Like the Bourbons, they have learnt nothing and forgotten nothing. Every year that passes, it becomes clearer that the invasion of 2003 was the defining calamity of the post-Cold War era.

The scale of the disaster can be measured not only by its direct victims – American, British, and above all, Iraqi. It must also be measured in the destruction of Iraqi society and the unleashing of new threats to the world order, threats much more real than Saddam's quite ordinary weaponry. Iraq's decade of civil war has had an appalling effect on the country's many minorities, some of which had been protected under Saddam. The number of Christians in the country, for instance (Iraq contains one of the oldest Christian communities in the world), has fallen from approximately 1.5 million in 2003 to perhaps 250,000 or fewer today.[4]

We can now see that the toppling of Saddam Hussein created a power vacuum that was swiftly filled by al-Qaeda in Iraq. Al-Qaeda in due course became the progenitor of Islamic State (IS). Although IS has drawn its mutant Islamist ideology from Saudi Arabian sources, its military and organizational strength evolved in al-Qaeda's war against US occupiers in the aftermath of 2003. Many Islamic State commanders, including its emir, Abu Bakr al-Baghdadi, learnt their fighting skills during the US occupation.

Spawned in Iraq, Islamic State has now spread across the Middle East and North Africa. As IS and its supporters carry

---

4   Source http://www.economist.com/blogs/erasmus/2014/07/iraqi-christians-and-west.

out atrocities in Europe and around the globe, it has become the most feared terror threat in the world.

This book maintains that the invasion of Iraq was responsible for launching a new epoch of horror, instability and violence across the globe. It asks how and why did Britain get involved in such a mistaken enterprise.

Crucially, this was a war of choice: there was no threat to Britain worthy of the name from Saddam Hussein's Iraq.

At the prime minister's private meeting on Iraq on 23 July 2002, Jack Straw was minuted as saying: 'It seemed clear that Bush had made up his mind to take military action, even if the timing was not yet decided. But the case was thin. Saddam was not threatening his neighbours, and his WMD capability was less than that of Libya, North Korea or Iran.'[5]

Despite such reservations Britain chose to support the US. We could have stood aside, as did France and Germany, on the grounds that al-Qaeda was the real enemy – an enemy that was also opposed by Iraq.

That, of itself, might have persuaded the US at least to pause before invading Iraq. The invasion faced significant opposition from American voters, within Congress and within the US military and even the Bush administration itself.[6] Tony Blair had high

---

5   The minute of the meeting was leaked in 2005. 'Blair Planned Iraq War from Start', *The Sunday Times*, 1 May 2005. Actually Iran had no WMD capability in 2002, and still has none. So much for the reliability of Joint Intelligence Assessments. In 2002, Libya and North Korea had chemical weapons but not nuclear weapons.
6   Doves included the chairman of Bush's Foreign Intelligence Advisory Board, Brent Scowcroft, the former CENTCOM commander, Anthony Zinni, and the chairman of the House Armed Services Committee, Ike Skelton. http://europe.newsweek.com/iraq-war-bushs-biggest-blunder-294411.

influence in the United States after 9/11 because of his warm expressions of solidarity with Britain's ally. As an opponent of invasion, he might have made a difference. Instead, he signed up to the neoconservative agenda of regime change through military force. In fairness, he did persuade the Bush administration to try to achieve this in an international coalition backed with the authority of the United Nations. But the UN process had an unexpected result. It gave no pretext to invade Iraq and demonstrated the absence of any international consensus to overthrow Saddam. When finally compelled to choose between the UN and the US, Blair chose the US. He *insisted* on Britain actually joining the invasion and the occupation, which transformed Iraq from an al-Qaeda-free zone into an area where al-Qaeda and its progeny flourish.

THE CHILCOT INQUIRY AND
THE BRITISH ESTABLISHMENT

Why and how did Britain get this all so wrong? In 2009 Prime Minister Gordon Brown announced that Sir John Chilcot, a retired civil servant, would chair an inquiry into the Iraq War with a view to learning lessons that could be applied in future conflicts.

Brown told the House of Commons that it would take a year for Sir John to carry out his work.[7] In the event the inquiry has

---

7   *Hansard*, House of Commons Debates, 15 June 2009, col 24.

taken more than six years and, in the spring of 2016, there was still no certainty when it will publish its report. Sir John and his colleagues became bogged down in arguments about which documents could be cited and published.[8]

As his inquiry has dragged on, British forces have been involved in fresh foreign engagements in Libya and Syria, carrying out bombing missions in both countries, as well as being drawn back into Iraq. The lessons of Iraq would have been relevant in all these cases.

The delay in completing the Chilcot Inquiry, combined with obvious defects in previous inquiries – four inquiries into these matters have come and gone – suggest that the British Establishment may be structurally incapable of addressing the very serious questions emerging from the invasion of Iraq. This is because the scale of the calamity raises existential questions that are too subversive to address.

The most important of these heart-of-the-matter issues concerns Britain's alliance with the United States. This has been at the core of our foreign policy since the Second World War. More than anything else, Tony Blair's determination to stick with the American president of the day, whoever he is and whatever he stands for, explains his willingness to follow the United States all the way into the Iraq morass.

Despite what his critics have claimed, Mr Blair's allegiance

---

8   For example, lengthy negotiations centred on records of telephone conversations between Mr Blair and President Bush. Twenty-nine written notes from Mr Blair to President Bush were eventually deemed publishable though even these were subject to redactions as the Iraq Inquiry website stated. http://www.iraqinquiry.org.uk/faq.aspx.

to the United States was by no means dishonourable. Britain is a nuclear power that depends heavily on US-supplied technology and operational support. Our place on the United Nations Security Council ultimately depends on US patronage.[9] The foreign intelligence service MI6 – deeply implicated in the Iraq invasion – intensely values its status as the closest and most trusted partner of its much better-resourced and far more powerful American counterpart, the CIA. Meanwhile, almost all rising British politicians take care to develop transatlantic connections. It has become axiomatic that the British military, diplomatic, political and intelligence establishments should support this 'special relationship' with the United States. The British state is ready to surrender its freedom of action on the international stage in return for the enhanced status and capability we derive as a result of our close US ties.

It is for this reason that the British military, Whitehall and the Secret Intelligence Service supported Tony Blair as Britain joined the United States' invasion of Iraq.

This book will show how the Iraq catastrophe has had a ruinous effect on these powerful and hugely respected institutions. The British army, having suffered two of the most damaging defeats in its history, has been left bereft of purpose. Giant questions surround the integrity, and even the patriotism, of the Secret Intelligence Service, an organization whose loyalty has never before been seriously called into question, even during its

---

9   Though it should be said that Britain's place on the UNSC is written into the UN charter. Britain could veto any attempt to deprive it of permanent membership of the council.

lowest point in the Cold War with the defection of the Cambridge spies in the 1950s.

The Iraq invasion damaged the core institutions of the British state. This in turn has led to basic questions about the British system of government itself. According to the textbooks the British state is a constitutional monarchy. This bland formula conceals the fact that the British state contains pre-modern elements, which enable a great deal of government to be carried out in secret.

Parliament had wrested away power from the monarchy over the centuries. But the precise nature of these powers has never been codified, as it would in a country with a written constitution. In practice this means that the executive branch of government inherited very significant residual powers from the monarchy.

As a consequence, there has always been an unresolved contradiction between an essentially medieval system of government and Britain's democratic tradition as it evolved over the last two hundred years. Prior to Iraq this contradiction had rarely become a live political issue – the British governing elite had hitherto been assumed to be honest, decent and disposed to act in the national interest.

The Iraq invasion, however, showed British officials in a different light. When the spotlight was turned on them in the aftermath of the invasion, it emerged that many of Britain's most senior officials had not conducted themselves with the integrity expected of public servants. Many were exposed as cheats or incompetents whose loyalty was given not to the British state, but to a partisan group of politicians and to their own careers.

It is depressingly clear that no key decision-maker in the

British state was rewarded for making a correct judgement about Iraq, and that no one who made a bad judgement, or colluded with one, has suffered any penalty. In the chapters that follow we will forensically examine the accuracy of public statements made by British officials and politicians about Iraq's so-called weapons of mass destruction. This book will make a judgement about the legality of the war. It will then go on to calculate the political consequences of the decision to go to war. In order to understand these grave issues, we need to go back in time and provide a brief history of Iraq and its relations with the West, and why the United States and Britain felt it was so important to intervene in 2003.

TWO

IRAQ AND THE WEST,
1979–2000

---

*'I was not an enthusiast about getting
US forces and going into Iraq.'*

Dick Cheney[10]

L ike so many Middle Eastern countries, Iraq is a British invention. We drew the boundaries of the country in the wake of
the collapse of the Ottoman Empire at the end of the First World
War, and thereafter kept an eye on it, mainly because of the oil.

The 1979 coup d'état formalized the power that Saddam
Hussein had in truth been wielding from behind the scenes for
more than a decade. Saddam's regime was always a ruthless one-
party dictatorship with an intense personality cult, and appalling

---

10   Interviewed by PBS *Frontline*, 28 January 1997.

human rights abuses. It cracked down especially hard on the Kurds in the north and on Iraq's Shia majority. However, Saddam's internal repression did not prevent the Western powers from doing business with him – particularly France, which helped him build a nuclear research reactor at Osiraq, which was subsequently knocked out by the Israelis in June 1981 in a daring bombing raid.

Saddam was initially estranged from the United States after President Carter negotiated the Camp David accords between Egypt and Israel in 1978. Seeking influence in the Arab world, he gave ostentatious leadership in the Arab League to the rejectionists, and secured Egypt's expulsion. Saddam played host to the ruthless Palestinian group led by Abu Nidal, and used it as a team of mercenary assassins to strike at the mainstream PLO and other targets. But after the Iranian revolution in 1979 the US and Saddam drew much closer, both governments identifying Ayatollah Khomeini as the enemy.

In September 1980 Saddam invaded Iran without condemnation or intervention from the Carter administration. After initial successes, Saddam's assault was beaten back and the Iranians counter-attacked. The Iranian Revolutionary Guard was far better motivated than Saddam's conscript armies and was willing to take heavy losses in human wave attacks. By July 1982 the Iranians had reconquered all their lost territory and launched a counter-invasion.

Saddam's forces used poison gas in desperate efforts to repel them. While the new Reagan administration made no public response, covertly it supported Iraq, especially through intelligence and logistics. It also authorized the sale to Iraq of items usable in chemical or biological warfare.[11] The Iraqis continued to do badly on the ground and in November 1983 Reagan issued a secret directive for his administration to take any measures necessary to prevent Saddam from losing the war.

Reagan even sent a special envoy to Saddam to offer further assistance and a pathway to full diplomatic relations (suspended since 1967). Of all people, this was Donald Rumsfeld, later the US defense secretary who would come to promote and organize the eventual overthrow of Saddam.[12] The State Department removed Iraq from its list of State Sponsors of Terrorism, paving the way for diplomatic relations to be restored in November 1984.

In the same year, President Reagan promoted a one-sided arms embargo against Iran. In the UK, the Thatcher government officially supported the UN embargo on arms supplies to both sides, but Mrs Thatcher's foreign secretary announced the 'Howe guidelines' distinguishing between lethal and non-lethal supplies. In practice, these allowed the export of some important secret supplies to Iraq, including agents for the manufacture of chemical weapons.[13]

The war settled into a terrible bloody stalemate, causing hundreds of thousands of military and civilian casualties on both sides, but US–Iraq relations continued to improve, seemingly regardless

---

11   See 'How Did Iraq Get Its Weapons? We Sold Them', *Sunday Herald* (Scotland), 8 September 2002.

12   See 'Shaking Hands with Saddam Hussein', National Security Archive Electronic Briefing Book no. 82, published by George Washington University, 25 February 2003.

13   For the official account of British policy during the Iran–Iraq War, see the government statement dated 15 February 1996, 'Government Policy on the Control of Exports to Iran and Iraq 1980 to 1990 – The Facts'.

of events on the ground. In March 1988 the Iraqis attacked the Kurdish town of Halabja with poison gas and nerve agents, as part of a parallel war against Kurdish insurgents. The attack killed up to 5,000 people and another 10,000 were seriously injured or maimed.

Although Halabja would come to figure prominently in the UK's 'September dossier' against Saddam in 2002, at the time it drew no condemnation from Western governments. (Apart from the work of a few obscure Iraqi exiles and their academic supporters, there was a strange silence in Britain and the United States about this pitiless regime.) A month after the Halabja atrocity, the United States continued to give intelligence and material support to the successful Iraqi attack on the Iranian occupiers of the strategic al-Fao peninsula, which included the use of cyanide and nerve gas.

The war at last came to an end in August 1988, with a ceasefire based on UN Security Council (UNSC) Resolution 598. This more or less restored the status quo as it had existed before Saddam had launched his invasion. Both sides had suffered vast human and economic losses, with Iraq owing enormous financial debts to other Arab states, including its small neighbour Kuwait. Iraq had never accepted Kuwaiti independence (proclaimed in 1961) and some regimes before Saddam's had claimed the state as a province of Iraq. After his failure in the Iran–Iraq War Saddam had both political and economic motives to confront Kuwait. Relations between the two countries deteriorated sharply when Kuwait refused to forgive Saddam's debt and frustrated his efforts within OPEC to drive up the price of oil. Saddam's language against Kuwait grew even more threatening in 1990 when he accused the Kuwaitis of stealing Iraq's oil through slant-wise drilling from its own territory, a complaint he referred to the US State Department.

The American ambassador met Saddam as his threats escalated. What transpired at the meeting remains in dispute even now, but many authorities have suggested that Saddam viewed it as a green light to seize Kuwait.[14]

Last-minute talks between Iraq and Kuwait were unproductive and on 2 August 100,000 Iraqi troops invaded Kuwait and occupied the whole country in a matter of hours. Even then, President George H. W. Bush was slow to respond. However, after being prodded by Margaret Thatcher (who was attending a conference with the president at Aspen, Colorado[15]) he told a press conference on 5 August: 'this will not stand, this aggression against Kuwait', and he referred to Saddam's regime as 'international outlaws and renegades'.[16] Just a few days earlier, Saddam had been in good standing with the United States.

THE FIRST GULF WAR

On the day of the invasion, the UN Security Council passed Resolution 660 condemning the occupation and demanding immediate Iraqi withdrawal. This was followed by Resolution

---

14   See for example Edward Mortimer in the *New York Review of Books*, 22 November 1990.

15   See Margaret Thatcher, *The Downing Street Years*, HarperCollins, 1993, pp. 816–20.

16   Transcript of President Bush exchange with reporters on the Iraqi invasion of Kuwait, 5 August 1990, http://www.margaretthatcher.org/document/110704.

661 which imposed a strict trade embargo on Iraq, enforced by a naval blockade authorized by Resolution 665. On the military front, Saudi Arabia shifted its policy of forbidding foreign intrusion in the land of Islam's holy places, and allowed a US military build-up on its soil. By October, Operation Desert Shield had amassed 200,000 US troops in Saudi Arabia and the Gulf states, supported by 15,000 British and 11,000 French soldiers. Meanwhile, Saddam – having initially flirted with creating a puppet government – annexed Kuwait as the nineteenth province of Iraq. The occupation was brutal and oppressive – however, it would later emerge that several reported Iraqi atrocities were in fact invented by imaginative Kuwaitis.[17]

On 29 November 1990 the UN Security Council (under American prompting) adopted Resolution 678, setting a deadline of 15 January 1991 for total Iraqi withdrawal from Kuwait. It gave UN members authority to use 'all necessary means' to achieve this objective. (Just a day earlier, Margaret Thatcher had resigned her premiership and was succeeded by John Major: this made no difference to British policy.)

On 9 January US Secretary of State James Baker met his Iraqi counterpart, Foreign Minister Tariq Aziz, in Geneva for last-minute talks, but these made no headway. By now, coalition forces had built up to nearly a million-strong: 697,000 US, 100,000 Saudi, over 45,000 British, and smaller contributions from twenty-six other

---

17 The American public relations firm Hill & Knowlton represented 'Citizens for a Free Kuwait', since described as 'a classic PR front group designed to hide the real role of the Kuwaiti government and its collusion with the Bush administration'. See J. Sauber and S. Rampton, *Toxic Sludge is Good for You*, Common Courage Press, 1995, p. 169.

countries, including Syria, Morocco and four other Arab states.[18] On 17 January the coalition launched Operation Desert Storm to expel Iraq from Kuwait. The plans – prepared by the chairman of the US Joint Chiefs of Staff, Colin Powell, and the local commander in the Gulf General Norman Schwarzkopf – were based on the early use of overwhelming force against the Iraqis. The troop numbers were far higher than those used twelve years later in the more mobile 'shock and awe' campaign devised by Donald Rumsfeld and imposed on a largely reluctant armed forces leadership.

Operation Desert Storm began with massive attacks on Saddam's air force and air defence systems. Saddam launched counter missile attacks on Israel and Saudi Arabia and occupied a small piece of Saudi territory, but the coalition plans continued relentlessly. On 22 January Saddam prepared for withdrawal from Kuwait by ordering the destruction of Kuwaiti oil wells. On 24 February coalition forces crossed into Kuwait. Thousands of Iraqi soldiers were killed as they retreated into Iraq. On 27 February Iraq announced that it would comply with all the relevant UN resolutions and President George H. W. Bush announced that the war was over. The following day a ceasefire came into effect. There are still strong disputes about the casualties on both sides, but there is no doubt that those of Iraqi fatalities, military and civilian, massively outnumbered those of the allies, even accepting the largest estimate of Kuwaiti casualties under the Iraqi occupation.

The ceasefire was formalized by UNSC Resolution 687, passed

---

18   See 'Military Statistics – Gulf War Coalition Forces (most recent) by country', http://www.nationmaster.com/country-info/stats/Military/Gulf-War-Coalition-Forces.

on 3 April and accepted by Iraq three days later. It demanded that Iraq recognize Kuwait, account for missing Kuwaitis, return stolen Kuwaiti property and end all support for international terrorism. It also called for Iraq to abandon chemical and biological weapons and ballistic missiles with a range greater than 150km. All existing stocks, agents, components and facilities related to such weapons were to be destroyed or removed, and a special commission called UNSCOM was created to supervise this.

Saddam's overwhelming defeat led to uprisings against his regime by the Shias in the south and the Kurds in the north. Both uprisings received encouragement from President Bush and they hoped for US support. But these hopes were soon destroyed under the brutal suppression of Saddam's surviving forces as the coalition looked on.[19] Eventually, US, British and French troops set up a safe haven for the Kurds in the north.

Neoconservatives later denounced President George H. W. Bush's decision to leave Saddam in power, so it is interesting to read the rationale for this decision by his defense secretary, Dick Cheney, who as vice-president to Bush's son a decade later would be a major advocate of the invasion of Iraq. Speaking in 1997, Cheney stressed:

> I was not an enthusiast about getting US forces and going into Iraq. We were there in the southern part of Iraq to the extent we needed to be there to defeat his forces and to get him out of Kuwait but the idea of going into Baghdad for example or trying

---

19 See 'Did the US betray Iraqis in 1991?', 7 April 2003, http://edition.cnn.com/2003/ALLPOLITICS/04/07/timep.betray.tm/.

to topple the regime wasn't anything I was enthusiastic about. I felt there was a real danger here that you would get bogged down in a long drawn-out conflict, that this was a dangerous, difficult part of the world. If you recall, we were all worried about the possibility of Iraq coming apart ... You're going to find yourself in a situation where you've redefined your war aims and now set up a new war aim that in effect would detract from the enormous success you just had. What we set out to do was to liberate Kuwait and destroy [Saddam's] offensive capability ... That was the mission I was given by the President. That's what we did.[20]

A year later, George H. W. Bush himself defended his decision in a joint article with his former National Security Adviser Brent Scowcroft:

We were disappointed that Saddam's defeat did not break his hold on power, as many of our Arab allies had predicted and we had come to expect. President Bush repeatedly declared that the fate of Saddam Hussein was up to the Iraqi people [Bush referred to himself in the third person].[21] Occasionally, he indicated that removal of Saddam would be welcome, but for very practical reasons there was never a promise to aid an uprising. While we

---

20   Dick Cheney, former defense secretary, interview for PBS *Frontline*, 28 January 1997.

21   President Bush also declared that the US wouldn't lift sanctions against Iraq while Saddam Hussein was in power, as did representatives of the Clinton administration throughout the 1990s – see http://david-morrison.org.uk/iraq/b-liar-e1.pdf, Annex D, p. 27 for a list of statements to that effect, beginning with one by Bush in May 1991, a matter of weeks after the disarmament Resolution 687 was passed, which promised that sanctions would be lifted if Iraq disarmed.

hoped that popular revolt or a coup would topple Saddam, neither the US nor the countries of the region wished to see the
break-up of the Iraqi state. We were concerned about the long-
term balance of power at the head of the Gulf. Trying to eliminate
Saddam, extending the ground war into an occupation of Iraq ...
would have incurred incalculable human and political costs ...
We would have been forced to occupy Baghdad and in effect rule
Iraq. The coalition would instantly have collapsed, the Arabs
deserting it in anger and other allies pulling out as well. Under
those circumstances, furthermore, we had been self-consciously
trying to set a pattern for handling aggression in the post-Cold
War world. Going in and occupying Iraq, thus unilaterally
exceeding the UN's mandate, would have destroyed the precedent
of international response to aggression we hoped to establish.[22]

This was a cogent statement of the multilateralist, pragmatic,
managerial approach to international security favoured at that
time by the US foreign policy establishment. This approach was
rejected – at times insultingly – by the younger Bush's administration, with the enthusiastic support of Tony Blair.

CONTAINMENT 1991–2001

The Security Council required Saddam Hussein to disarm
'under international supervision'. This presented Saddam with a

---

22   George H. W. Bush and Brent Scowcroft, 'Why We Didn't Remove Saddam',
     Time, 2 March 1998.

dilemma he failed to resolve. On the one hand, he had to satisfy the Western powers that he was disarming to have any hope of escaping isolation and sanctions – and to avoid creating another pretext to attack him and depose him. But on the other hand, he needed the Iranians and his internal enemies to continue believing that he still possessed chemical and biological weapons. This led him into a confused and profitless policy of fitful confrontations with the inspection regime while secretly destroying huge stocks of weapons. Saddam followed this policy to the very outbreak of war in 2003, still attempting to juggle the West's demands for proof that he had disarmed while hoping to bluff the Iranians that he had not.[23]

In August 1991, despite their dissatisfaction with Saddam's co-operation with UNSCOM, the Western powers adopted a twin-track approach to disarmament under UNSC Resolutions 706 and 707. The first set up a programme under the banner of 'Humanitarian Aid', allowing Iraq to export a limited

---

23   According to a remarkable book by the American investigative journalist Ron Suskind, Saddam's intelligence chief, Tahir Jalil Habbush, delivered this message to the MI6 officer Michael Shipster on the eve of war. He told Shipster that Iraq had destroyed all its WMD. Shipster was examined privately, with other MI6 officers, by the Chilcot Inquiry. See R. Suskind, *The Way of the World*, Harper, 2008. One of Suskind's sources, Nigel Inkster, subsequently described the comments attributed to him in the book as being 'inaccurate and misleading'. Lynne Jones MP has since pointed out that 'The sources of that information – Richard Dearlove and Nigel Inkster – have queried the exact recollection of those conversations, but they have not denied the substance of the allegation that one of our top agents obtained information that Saddam Hussein had no weapons of mass destruction. It would appear that that intelligence was ignored.' See the postscript to 'Angry denials are not enough', August 6, 2008, http://www.theguardian.com/commentisfree/2008/aug/06/iraq.iraq and *Hansard*, House of Commons Debates, 25 March 2009, Col 361.

amount of oil with the proceeds paid into an escrow account intended to pay for food, medicines and other essential supplies; the second demanded that Iraq give immediate and unconditional access to weapons inspectors from UNSCOM and the International Atomic Energy Agency (IAEA). The latter was reinforced by UNSC Resolution 715, presenting specific monitoring and verification plans, which Iraq immediately declared to be unlawful.

In August 1995 Saddam's son-in-law, Hussein Kamal, defected to Jordan and provided new revelations of clandestine lethal weapons programmes. In addition, Kamal told CNN that all proscribed weapons had been destroyed, prompting fresh disclosures by Saddam.[24] Kamal and his family were enticed back into Iraq and immediately executed.

The regime then took a series of steps to consolidate its power. Saddam's son Uday supervised the execution of over 400 officers accused of plotting a coup. Saddam staged a referendum winning 99.96 per cent support for another seven years in power. In 1996 he launched an assault against the Kurds in the north, recapturing the city of Irbil. The United States retaliated in the south, with Cruise missile attacks and an extension of the no-fly zone to a point just south of Baghdad. Meanwhile, Iraq clashed repeatedly with the UNSCOM inspectors as they adopted more confrontational tactics of surprise visits to suspected facilities.

In November 1996 President Bill Clinton won a comfortable re-election victory against Republican veteran Bob Dole. Clinton

---

24 See the transcript of the CNN interview at http://edition.cnn.com/WORLD/
9509/iraq_defector/kamel_transcript/index.html.

appointed Madeleine Albright as the first female secretary of state, but there followed no change in Iraq policy. Albright announced in March 1997 that sanctions were likely to continue until Saddam was gone. When the regime continued to block UNSCOM inspections she promoted the tough Security Council Resolution 1115 to reinforce his obligations to allow unrestricted access to sites and officials. In July the Australian Richard Butler became the new head of UNSCOM. Butler pursued a yet more confrontational approach, particularly in seeking access to Saddam's network of palaces. Saddam retaliated by ordering the expulsion of all American inspectors, which led to the complete withdrawal of UNSCOM in November 1997.

President Clinton then drew up plans for military action against Iraq with his new British partner Tony Blair, who had won a landslide general election victory in May 1997 to displace the stale and scandal-struck administration of John Major. Blair signalled that moral judgements as well as conventional assessments of national interest would play a part in British policy. It is worth noting, however, that Blair had never once raised Iraq in the House of Commons as leader of the opposition, despite widespread evidence of Saddam's rule by fear and violence.

Clinton's plans were averted in February 1998 when UN Secretary-General Kofi Annan made a deal with Saddam Hussein. Saddam agreed to the return of the weapons inspectors and promised complete compliance with all relevant UN resolutions. This agreement was endorsed by UNSC Resolution 1154. But the regime and UNSCOM soon had a series of further clashes: over the discovery of missiles which had allegedly been filled with the chemical agent VX; over inspections of eight presidential palaces; and over Iraq's 'inadequate' declarations on biological weapons. In August, Tariq Aziz tried to force Butler to declare Iraq free of weapons of mass destruction. Butler refused and again Iraq withdrew all co-operation with UNSCOM.

REGIME CHANGE AND DESERT FOX

Against this background of renewed confrontation, the US Congress passed the Iraq Liberation Act in October 1998, which made it US public policy to seek the replacement of Saddam Hussein with a democratic regime. It obliged Clinton to designate various Iraqi exile groups as potential replacements, although given Saddam's repression none had been able to establish any following within Iraq. Indeed many of their members had not set foot in the country for decades.

The main promoters of the Iraq Liberation Act were neoconservative Republicans, particularly the think tank and pressure group, the Project for the New American Century, which would supply Paul Wolfowitz and other important members of the future Bush administration. The project's agenda stressed 'American global leadership' through greatly increased defence spending and assertive unilateral policies.[25] Clinton did little to resist their demands. He had lost control of Congress in 1994 and in 1998 he personally was mired in the Lewinsky scandal. However,

---

25   See Project for the New American Century, 'Statement of Principles', 3 June 1997.

he managed to keep the demand for regime change on the back burner for the remainder of his second term.

In November 1998 Clinton ordered air strikes against Iraq. They were called off when Iraq renewed promises to co-operate fully with UNSCOM. In December there was a further stand-off which led to the withdrawal of all UNSCOM and IAEA weapons inspectors. It became accepted wisdom that Saddam had ordered their expulsion but Butler later revealed that he had withdrawn the UNSCOM staff on advice from Washington.[26]

On 16 December Clinton and Blair launched Operation Desert Fox, a three-day campaign of air strikes against 100 supposed WMD sites. The official rationale was Saddam's failure to provide full access to weapons inspectors: cynics remarked that the operation was launched on the very day that Clinton was impeached over the Lewinsky affair.

There remains a mystery about Operation Desert Fox. It was not justified by any secret rearmament by Saddam. Quite the contrary: almost a year earlier, Britain's Joint Intelligence Committee reckoned that 'UNSCOM and the IAEA have succeeded in destroying or controlling the vast majority of Saddam's 1991 weapons of mass destruction (WMD) capability.'[27]

A key question therefore is this: why did the US and UK engage in a bombing campaign in December 1998, when UK intelligence assessed that Iraq had very little in the way of 'weapons of mass destruction'? Perhaps, it was to ensure that the inspectors

---

26   See R. Butler, *Saddam Defiant*, Weidenfeld and Nicolson, 2000, p. 224.
27   See 'The Butler Review of Intelligence on Weapons of Mass Destruction', 2004, paragraph 181, https://fas.org/irp/world/uk/butler071404.pdf.

wouldn't be let back in – thereby making it impossible to give Iraq a completely clean bill of health, which would lead in turn to international calls for the abandonment of sanctions?[28]

Blair claimed success for the operation and asserted 'we have severely damaged Saddam's ability to produce and repair ballistic missiles. We have severely set back his chemical, biological and unmanned drone programmes.'[29] Years later Blair's claim of success was repudiated by two senior intelligence officials, Dr Brian Jones and John Morrison, on the BBC's *Panorama* programme: Morrison was subsequently dismissed from his post as adviser to the House of Commons Intelligence and Security Committee.[30] Blair himself, however, disavowed his own claims in 2010 when he published his memoirs: 'The operation was a limited success. The general feeling was that Saddam had got away with it again.'[31]

Operation Desert Fox was opposed by three of the five permanent members of the Security Council, Russia, China and France, and its legality was disputed. Clinton and Blair relied on UNSC Resolution 1154: they argued that Saddam's breach of the resolution was a matter of fact and that they had the authority to enforce it without further deliberation in the Security Council – a rehearsal of the argument ultimately used to justify the invasion of Iraq.

Russia, China and France pushed for the replacement of UNSCOM and this was achieved in December 1999 by the

---

28 For a full analysis of Operation Desert Fox and its likely purpose see http:// david-morrison.org.uk/iraq/b-liar-e1.pdf, Annex D, p. 27.

29 See 'Saddam is Back in His Cage, says Blair', *The Herald* (Scotland), 21 December 1998

30 'A Failure of Intelligence', *Panorama*, 9 July 2004.

31 T. Blair, *A Journey*, Arrow, 2011, p. 222.

establishment of a new inspection regime, the Monitoring, Verification and Inspection Commission (UNMOVIC). UNSC Resolution 1284 demanded full co-operation with this new body. Iraq rejected this, because it did not meet its call for the relaxation of sanctions. No inspectors returned to Iraq and in February 2000 Clinton and Blair ordered another series of bombing raids. After some months of disagreement, the Security Council had found a chairman for UNMOVIC, Dr Hans Blix, the former Swedish foreign minister and head of the International Atomic Energy Agency.

In November 2000, after a knife-edge election result, George W. Bush defeated Clinton's vice-president Al Gore (who secured more of the popular vote in the election) to become the new president of the United States. Bush inherited from Bill Clinton a formal commitment to achieve regime change in Iraq and an actual policy which left the regime in power. In February 2001 Blair joined with the new president in ordering a new series of bombing raids.

Containment, sanctions and inspections had eliminated Saddam's ability to threaten any other country – but without providing the certainty that he had disarmed. The limitations of the containment regime allowed the neoconservatives – with Tony Blair's support – to exploit the spectre of a ruthless dictator, in imminent or actual possession of horribly destructive weapons, with lethal ambitions against the Western world.

However, the neoconservatives still needed their opportunity. On 11 September 2001 their moment came. Al-Qaeda's attack on the United States provided the perfect pretext for finally getting rid of Saddam.

ASSAULT ON AFGHANISTAN

Tony Blair's instant response to 9/11 was perfectly judged. He promised to stand 'shoulder to shoulder' with the United States. Within days he was flying to meet President Bush in Washington, where he heard him for the first time use the words 'war on terror'. He sat in the gallery to hear the US president address Congress. The president looked up and said: 'Thank you for coming, friend.'

Tony Blair was of some assistance to Colin Powell as he successfully persuaded Bush to concentrate initially on expelling al-Qaeda and the Taliban government which had sheltered them from Afghanistan. But the hawks in the Bush administration continually urged the president also to settle accounts with Saddam. Several years later, the then British ambassador Sir Christopher Meyer claimed that Bush told Blair privately that when Afghanistan was finished 'we must come back to Iraq'.[32]

The assault on Afghanistan began on 7 October with a massive aerial bombardment.[33] By November Osama Bin Laden was trapped in the wild Tora Bora mountains of eastern Afghanistan, near the porous border with Pakistan. However most of the ground fighting was outsourced to anti-Taliban Afghan warlords in the so-called Northern Alliance, which enabled Bin Laden and most Taliban leaders to escape.

The Bush administration had no enthusiasm for a long-term

---

32 See 'Bush and Blair Made Secret Pact for Iraq War', *Guardian*, 4 April 2004.
33 Authorized by the United Nations Security Council, in contrast to Kosovo and Desert Fox and the 2003 invasion of Iraq.

nation-building effort in Afghanistan. After expelling its enemies, it was quick to hand over responsibility for security to a
UN-sponsored international force, supporting a provisional government headed by a favoured local politician, Hamid Karzai, but
also heavily dependent on regional warlords. Later the Americans
would pour troops back into Afghanistan. Eventually their numbers surged to nearly 100,000. But for the time being, the Bush
administration could now turn on the enemies who mattered
most to them.

In his State of the Union speech on 29 January 2002 Bush star-
tled most of his allies when he named Iraq, Iran and North Korea
as 'an axis of evil, arming to threaten the peace of the world'.

He claimed that Iraq continued to 'flaunt its hostility toward
America and to support terror. The Iraqi regime has plotted to
develop anthrax and nerve gas and nuclear weapons for over a
decade.' He added:

> By seeking weapons of mass destruction these regimes pose a
> grave and growing danger. They could provide these arms to
> terrorists, giving them the means to match their hatred ... All
> nations should know: America will do what is necessary to
> ensure our nation's security. We'll be deliberate, yet time is not
> on our side. I will not wait on events while dangers gather.[34]

The United States now set about seeking allies for its attack on
Iraq. First among those allies was Britain.

---

34   George W. Bush, State of the Union Address, 29 January 2002.

THREE

THE SHIFT FROM AFGHANISTAN TO IRAQ

'We believe that the sanctions regime has effectively contained Saddam Hussein in the last ten years. During this time he has not attacked his neighbours, nor used chemical weapons against his own people.'

PRIME MINISTER TONY BLAIR[35]

In early 2002 George W. Bush suggested Tony Blair should visit him at his family ranch in Crawford, Texas. It was a flattering invitation. The British prime minister brought his family, including his mother-in-law, along with him. However, this was not a social call. The subject matter was serious: the US plan to invade Iraq.

Some well-placed observers believe that this meeting in

---

35   Written Answer, House of Commons, 1 November 2000.

Crawford, at the start of April 2002 and nearly a full year ahead of the actual invasion, marked the moment that Tony Blair began to commit Britain to invasion. They hold that the prime minister made a binding, though private pledge.[36]

The two leaders did indeed spend a great deal of time in private together. Most unusually, there were no advisers present. No notes were taken. This means that it is impossible to fathom exactly what, if anything, Tony Blair pledged to George W. Bush during his time at Crawford. There is, moreover, no hard evidence that a pledge was made. No secret treaty has come to light.

The discussions at Crawford did, however, bring into the open a gap between the United States and the British position. The United States was committed to regime change: it wanted to get rid of Saddam Hussein on the grounds that the world would be better off without him. This had been the openly declared position of the United States ever since the Iraq Liberation Act was passed in the late 1990s, and it was fervently supported by the neoconservatives around Bush.

There was one problem with this objective, however. Under international law, regime change is not, and never can be, grounds for the invasion of another country.

For George W. Bush and his circle of neoconservative advisers none of this mattered. As far as they were concerned international

---

36 The former British ambassador in Washington, Sir Christopher Meyer, told the Chilcot Inquiry he was 'not entirely clear what degree of convergence was ... signed in blood, at the Crawford ranch' but pointed to the 'clues in the speech which Tony Blair gave the next day' in which he mentioned 'regime change', Meyer thought, for the first time in public.
http://www.iraqinquiry.org.uk/media/40453/20091126am-final.pdf, p. 29.

law was a joke, a weapon used by weaker states to undermine US power. They were, furthermore, contemptuous of the United Nations, the designated guardian of international law.

Tony Blair also liked the idea of regime change. He agreed with his friend George W. Bush that Saddam Hussein was a monster. But Blair needed to find cover under international law. He needed this for two reasons. The first might be called traditional: all modern British governments, parliaments and essential institutions, including the armed forces, have professed adherence to the rule of law. For all his rhetoric of modernization, Blair could do no less. The second was political: he needed legal cover to carry the Labour Party into support for war.

This analysis explains a paradox which was to govern Tony Blair's conduct for the next ten months. In his conversations with President Bush, so far as we can tell, the British prime minister expressed strong support for regime change. On the other hand he seems to have made that support conditional through his insistence that Bush should seek legal mechanisms to secure the downfall of the Iraqi leader. That meant going through the United Nations, however much the neoconservatives despised the organization.

Documents later presented to the Chilcot Inquiry set out very clearly the background to the dialogue between Tony Blair and George W. Bush. On 12 March 2002 David Manning, Blair's chief foreign policy adviser, had a preliminary conversation with Condoleezza Rice, Bush's national security adviser, ahead of the Crawford summit. Manning told Rice that Blair 'would not budge in [his] support for regime change'. Five days later, on

17 March, Christopher Meyer, the UK's ambassador in Washington, met Deputy Secretary of Defense Paul Wolfowitz. Meyer repeated David Manning's message: Britain 'backed regime change but the plan had to be clever and failure was not an option'.[37]

On 25 March Foreign Secretary Jack Straw sent Blair a shrewd memorandum in advance of his imminent meeting with Bush. Straw warned Blair that Labour MPs were not ready to support an early military attack on Saddam. To provide legal cover and a plausible pretext for such action, Blair needed to present the elimination of Iraq's weapons of mass destruction capacity as its objective, rather than regime change. Blair should demand 'the unfettered readmission of weapons inspectors'.[38]

The evidence presented to Chilcot suggests that Tony Blair followed Straw's advice when he went to Crawford on 5 April: he would support military action by Bush *if* Saddam refused to accept the return of UN weapons inspectors.[39] Whatever the exact terms agreed at Crawford, Blair followed the same line of policy all the way up to the eve of the Iraq War itself.

To sum up: my contention is that Tony Blair committed himself to regime change in Iraq. He also committed himself to support US military action to achieve this. He was, however, genuinely

---

37 Meyer to Manning, 18 March 2002. The Manning and Meyer correspondence can be found in many sources: the most convenient is the Iraq Inquiry Digest website under the category 'The Downing Street Documents', http://www.iraqinquirydigest.org/?page_id=161. These documents were leaked to the journalist Michael Smith in 2004 and 2005.

38 Jack Straw, memorandum PM/02/019, 25 March 2002, declassified, published by the Chilcot Inquiry.

39 See in particular 'There is No Doubt About It: Tony Blair was on the Warpath from Early 2002', *Guardian*, 18 October 2015.

concerned that the Bush administration would initiate military action unilaterally rather than through an international coalition.

To secure that coalition – and to secure domestic support – Blair had to link military action with Saddam's compliance with UN resolutions. Beyond this, he needed to persuade the public to identify Saddam Hussein as an *urgent* threat. On his return to Britain he set about doing exactly that.

WEAPONS OF MASS DESTRUCTION

In the months that followed the meeting at the Crawford ranch Tony Blair and his team of advisers dedicated themselves to proving that Saddam Hussein was not just an evil monster – but also a monster hell-bent on the destruction of his neighbours.

Within weeks of Tony Blair's return from Crawford, Alastair Campbell, Downing Street director of communications, had a meeting with the chairman of the Joint Intelligence Committee John Scarlett and other Whitehall officials. In his diary he recorded the purpose of the meeting: 'to go through what we needed to do communications-wise to set the scene for Iraq, eg a WMD paper and other papers about Saddam'. Scarlett, recorded Campbell, was 'a very good bloke'.[40]

WMD was shorthand for 'weapons of mass destruction', a phrase that was starting to come into widespread use in official briefing and in the media. The term itself was not that new.

---

40   A. Campbell, *The Alastair Campbell Diaries, Vol. 4*, Hutchinson, 2012, p. 215.

Indeed it seems first to have been used by Cosmo Gordon Lang, Archbishop of Canterbury, following the German bombing of Guernica during the Spanish Civil War in the 1930s. However, it suddenly became ubiquitous as war with Iraq loomed. But what does the term WMD actually convey? The United Nations definition, set out in 1948, is very precise:

> ... atomic explosive weapons, radioactive material weapons, lethal chemical and biological weapons, and any weapons developed in the future which have characteristics comparable in destructive effect to those of the atomic bomb or other weapons mentioned above.[41]

WMD was a phrase resonant with menace, partly because of its novelty, and all the more terrifying because very few people were certain they knew what it really meant. From Tony Blair's point of view there was one gigantic problem with the neologism. It is a problem which still haunts him today: while there was plenty of evidence that Saddam Hussein was a bloodthirsty tyrant, there was no serious evidence that Saddam Hussein

---

41   Lord Butler's report sympathized 'with the view that, whatever its origin, the phrase and its accompanying abbreviation is now used so variously as to confuse rather than enlighten readers'. It therefore took as its definition paragraphs 8 and 9 of UNSCR 687 'which defined the systems which Iraq was required to abandon: "Nuclear weapons or nuclear-weapons-usable material or any subsystems or components or any research, development, support or manufacturing facilities ... Chemical and biological weapons and all stocks of agents and all related subsystems ...".' UNSCR 687 notably also included within its definition the means of WMD delivery: 'Ballistic missiles with a range greater than 150 kilometres and related major parts, and repair and production facilities'. Butler Review, 2004, pp. 3–4 https://fas.org/irp/world/uk/butler071404.pdf.

possessed viable 'weapons of mass destruction' that would pose any threat to his neighbours, let alone Britain. Nor was there any sign whatever that Saddam hoped to use any such weapons for a new campaign of conquest as opposed to deterrence and defence.

Furthermore, British officials were aware of the flimsy nature of the evidence, as testimony provided to the Chilcot Inquiry vividly demonstrates.

THE TESTIMONY OF CARNE ROSS

Carne Ross was a British diplomat who served as First Secretary for the Middle East at the UK Mission to the United Nations in New York from late 1997 to June 2002. Throughout this period he was responsible for Iraq policy, including policy on sanctions, weapons inspections and liaison with the weapons inspectors. There can have been few people in the government, if any, who knew more about Iraq and the level of threat it posed than Carne Ross. As he told Lord Butler in 2004 and subsequently repeated to the Chilcot Inquiry:

> I read the available UK and US intelligence on Iraq every work-
> ing day for the four and a half years of my posting. This daily
> briefing would often comprise a thick folder of material, both
> humint and sigint [i.e. human and signals intelligence]. I also
> talked often and at length about Iraq's WMD to the international

experts who comprised the inspectors of UNSCOM/UNMOVIC, whose views I would report to London. In addition, I was on many occasions asked to offer views in contribution to Cabinet Office assessments, including the famous WMD dossier (whose preparation began some time before my departure in June 2002).[42]

Ross also told Chilcot that when he was appointed to his job at the United Nations he received a briefing from the Foreign Office:

When I was briefed in London at the end of 1997 in preparation for my posting, I was told that we did not believe that Iraq had any significant WMD. The key argument therefore to maintain sanctions was that Iraq had failed to provide convincing evidence of destruction of its past stocks.

Iraq's ability to *launch* a WMD or any form of attack was very limited. There were approx twelve or so unaccounted-for Scud missiles; Iraq's airforce was depleted to the point of total ineffectiveness; its army was but a pale shadow of its earlier might; there was no evidence of any connection between Iraq and any terrorist organisation that might have planned an attack using Iraqi WMD (I do not recall any occasion when the question of a terrorist connection was even raised in UK/US discussions or UK internal debates).

There was moreover no intelligence or assessment during

---

42   Carne Ross, Testimony to the Iraq Inquiry, 12 July 2010, Annex A, 'Submission to the Butler Review', p. 13.

my time in the job that Iraq had any *intention* to launch an attack against its neighbours or the UK or US.[43] [Emphasis in original.]

Carne Ross's testimony is worth quoting at such length because he expresses with authority and precision the official position that Saddam Hussein's Iraq presented only a limited threat to its neighbours – and none at all to Britain and the United States. This was the common opinion at the start of 2002 in London, Washington and Moscow.[44] However, public assertions by the British prime minister told another story.

---

43 Ibid., p. 14.
44 See the memo from Peter Ricketts, Political Director to the Foreign Office, to Jack Straw, 22 March 2002: 'The truth is that what has changed is not the pace of Saddam Hussein's WMD programmes, but our tolerance of them post-11 September. ... But even the best survey of Iraq's WMD programmes will not show much advance in recent years on the nuclear, missile or CW/BW [chemical weapons/biological weapons] fronts: the programmes are extremely worrying but have not, as far as we know, been stepped up. US scrambling to establish a link between Iraq and al-Qa'eda is so far frankly unconvincing. To get public and Parliamentary support for military options we have to be convincing that: – the threat is so serious/imminent that it is worth sending our troops to die for.' This view was also held by Jack Straw himself, as we have seen in his minuted comments at a Downing Street meeting on 23 July 2002: 'It seemed clear that Bush had made up his mind to take military action, even if the timing was not yet decided. But the case was thin. Saddam was not threatening his neighbours, and his WMD capability was less than that of Libya, North Korea or Iran.' Minute of Downing Street meeting titled 'Iraq: Prime Minister's Meeting, 23 July' written by Matthew Rycroft, aide to David Manning. Documents as reproduced through the Iraq Inquiry Digest website. President Putin of Russia also held that opinion, as he stated during a tense joint press conference with Tony Blair on 11 October 2002: 'Russia does not have in its possession any trustworthy data that supports the existence of nuclear weapons or any weapons of mass destruction in Iraq and we have not received any such information from our partners as yet. This fact has also been supported by the information sent by the CIA to the US Congress.' See 'Putin Demands Proof over Iraqi Weapons', *Guardian*, 12 October 2002.

PUBLIC STATEMENTS FROM
TONY BLAIR ON WMD

From early 2002 onwards Tony Blair uttered a series of false and misleading statements about the existence and development of Iraq's so-called weapons of mass destruction.

On 3 April 2002, Blair told NBC News: 'We know that he [Saddam Hussein] has stockpiles of major amounts of chemical and biological weapons, we know that he is trying to acquire nuclear capability, we know that he is trying to develop ballistic missile capability of a greater range.'[45]

Three days later, at a press conference with President Bush, Tony Blair informed reporters that 'we know he has been developing these weapons. We know that those weapons constitute a threat.'[46]

Then on 10 April 2002, the prime minister said this in the House of Commons:

> Saddam Hussein's regime is despicable, he is developing weapons of mass destruction, and we cannot leave him doing so unchecked. He is a threat to his own people and to the region and, if allowed to develop these weapons, a threat to us also.[47]

It is today possible to compare these emphatic public

---

45 Tony Blair interviewed by Katie Couric, NBC News, 3 April 2002.
46 White House Press Release: 'President Bush, Prime Minister Blair Hold Press Conference', 6 April 2002.
47 Prime Minister's statement, *Hansard*, House of Commons Debates, 10 April 2002, col 23.

statements about the Iraqi threat (Blair made plenty of others) with the contemporaneous judgements made by the intelligence services. A summary of these was published in Lord Butler's 2004 review of the Iraq intelligence.

The Joint Intelligence Committee (JIC) assessments available to the prime minister in March were cautious. They emphasized how little was known about Iraqi weapons programmes, and stopped short of any definitive claims either way on the existence of stockpiles of weapons, or the development of them. The JIC assessment of 15 March 2002, for instance, stated:

> Intelligence on Iraq's weapons of mass destruction (WMD) and ballistic missile programmes is sporadic and patchy … From the evidence available to us, we believe Iraq retains some production equipment, and some small stocks of CW agent precursors, and may have hidden small quantities of agents and weapons … There is no intelligence on any BW agent production facilities but one source indicates that Iraq may have developed mobile production facilities.[48]

The discrepancies between the intelligence assessments made by the JIC and the statements of the prime minister are stark.

---

48 As quoted in the Butler Review, 2004, pp. 81, 167 and 69. See also the capable analysis carried out by Cambridge University's Glen Rangwala and the writer and campaigner Dan Plesch in their booklet *A Case to Answer, A First Report on the Potential Impeachment of the Prime Minister for High Crimes and Misdemeanours in Relation to the Invasion of Iraq*, Spokesman Books, 2004. This booklet compares public pronouncements by Tony Blair with underlying intelligence assessments as published in the Butler Review. It contains other examples of Tony Blair's bold pronouncements about Saddam Hussein's WMD.

While the JIC was suggesting that Iraq 'may have hidden small quantities of [chemical] agents and weapons', the prime minister was stating that 'we know that he has stockpiles of major amounts of chemical and biological weapons'.

The prime minister's false comments would have been to some extent forgivable if they reflected accurately what British intelligence assessments were telling him at the time.[49] But they did not. Tony Blair's statements to the media and Parliament were gross misrepresentations of the underlying intelligence produced by the JIC and available to him as prime minister.[50]

His statements about the threat from Saddam Hussein were profoundly misleading. They were also vital for making the case for war against Iraq. They provide the background to the announcement in early September 2002 that Downing Street was to publish a 'dossier' of Saddam Hussein's weapons of mass destruction.

---

49 Lord Butler stated in 2007 that 'neither the United Kingdom nor the United States had the intelligence that proved conclusively that Iraq had those weapons. The Prime Minister was disingenuous about that. The United Kingdom intelligence community told him on 23 August 2002 that, "we … know little about Iraq's chemical and biological weapons work since late 1988". The Prime Minister did not tell us that. Indeed, he told Parliament only just over a month later that the picture painted by our intelligence services was "extensive, detailed and authoritative". Those words could simply not have been justified by the material that the intelligence community provided to him.' Lords *Hansard*, 22 February 2007, Col 1231.

50 Blair told the Iraq Inquiry he had gone back over the 'vast number of different [intelligence] documents that refer to Saddam and WMD' that were made available to him during the period: 'I simply make the point that the assumption in all of them was that Saddam was committed in both the intent and the action in developing WMD.' Statement to the Iraq Inquiry, 14 January 2011.

THE SEPTEMBER DOSSIER

The September dossier had started life in February 2002 as a paper for public consumption on the mass destructive capabilities of four countries: Iran, Iraq, Libya and North Korea. All bar Libya had been cited as part of the 'axis of evil' in George W. Bush's notorious State of the Union speech a few weeks earlier.

Almost at once this dossier ran into problems. Foreign Secretary Jack Straw was concerned that there was nothing exceptional about Iraq's WMD capabilities. This raised the question: why take military action against Iraq rather than one of the others?

In a note to Tony Blair on 25 March the foreign secretary wrote that 'in the documents so far presented it has been hard to glean whether the threat from Iraq is so significantly different from that of Iran and North Korea as to justify military action'.[51]

In fact, of the four countries of concern in the original paper, the intelligence services considered Iraq to be in third or fourth place. It was not surprising therefore that Jack Straw was concerned that the four-country paper written for public consumption didn't focus sufficiently on Iraq. In a minute dated 11 March, he is quoted as commenting: 'Good, but should not Iraq be first and also have more text? The paper has to show

---

51   Straw also recognized that there was no evidence that Iraq had any part in 9/11: 'If 11 September had not happened, it is doubtful that the US would now be considering military action against Iraq. In addition, there has been no credible evidence to link Iraq with UBL [Osama bin Laden] and al Qaida. Objectively, the threat from Iraq has not worsened as a result of 11 September. …' Straw memorandum PM/02/019, 25 March 2002, declassified, published by the Iraq Inquiry.

why there is an exceptional threat from Iraq. It does not quite do this yet.'[52]

On 15 March, Chairman of the Joint Intelligence Committee John Scarlett helpfully suggested a solution to his problem:

> You may still wish to consider whether more impact could be achieved if the paper only covered Iraq. This would have the benefit of obscuring the fact that in terms of WMD, Iraq is not that exceptional.[53]

To be fair, John Scarlett did note that there were some 'unique features' about Iraq. Shortly after, John Scarlett's advice was taken when it was agreed that the paper for public consumption would focus on Iraq alone.[54] Thanks to John Scarlett's advice, the fact that Iraq's capability was *not exceptional* was duly *obscured*.

It was not until 3 September that Tony Blair announced that

---

52 Excerpt of minute from Simon McDonald to Peter Ricketts, 11 March 2002, titled Iraq, 'WMD Programmes of Concern', p. 43, as released under FOI305712.

53 Minute from Scarlett to Manning, 15 March 2002, 'WMD Programmes of Concern', p. 50.

54 A further sleight of hand proposed by Tim Dowse, head of counter proliferation at the Foreign and Commonwealth Office, was not implemented. In a letter to colleagues on 25 March (ibid., p. 73) headed 'Iraq: Material for Public Release', he proposed that the Defence Intelligence estimates of chemical precursors deemed unaccounted for in Iraq be expressed in a different manner, so that the fact that the estimates had been reduced would be obscured. He wrote: 'I realise that this would not in the end hoodwink a real expert, who would be able to reverse the calculation and work out that our assessment of precursor quantities had fallen. But the task would be ... impossible for a layman. And the result would, I think, have more impact on the target audience for [the] unclassified paper.'

While this enhancement wasn't implemented, it shows that telling the truth to the public about Iraq's weapons capabilities was not an absolute priority among civil servants dealing with the issue.

the government would publish his dossier of evidence that Iraq had weapons of mass destruction. Under pressure from the independent-minded Labour MP Graham Allen he agreed to recall Parliament from its long summer recess.[55] On 24 September Blair published the promised dossier. Subsequent inquiries would lay bare some of the secrets of its preparation and the way in which cautious intelligence statements had been rewritten as propaganda.

In the foreword to the dossier Blair stated firmly:

> What I believe the assessed intelligence has established beyond doubt is that Saddam has continued to produce chemical and biological weapons, that he continues in his efforts to develop nuclear weapons, and that he has been able to extend the range of his ballistic missile programme.[56]

Almost all of these assertions turned out to be misleading. Blair made one particularly discreditable claim: that 'some of these [chemical and biological] weapons are deployable within forty-five minutes of an order to use them'. We will examine this claim in Chapter 9.

Part three of the dossier made a moral case to act against Saddam by citing atrocities against his own people, without once mentioning that some of the worst of them had taken place when the Iraqi dictator had enjoyed Western support during his war with Iran. Meanwhile, Tony Blair's strategy was bearing fruit on another front.

---

55   Allen made preparations for a 'DIY recall' of MPs to debate Iraq and secured the agreement of the former Speaker Bernard Weatherill to chair this.

56   Foreword, 'Iraq's Weapons of Mass Destruction: The Assessment of the British Government', p. 3.

FOUR

THE ROAD TO WAR

*'There is an alternative to war:
disarming Iraq through inspections.'*

Dominique de Villepin, Speech to the United
Nations Security Council, 14 February 2003

Tony Blair had urged George W. Bush to go down the United Nations route at Crawford. By the autumn he had succeeded.

On 12 September the US president addressed the UN General Assembly. He asked other world leaders to confront the 'grave and gathering danger' of Iraq – or stand aside for the United States to act alone. Crucially, he gave Saddam a final chance to comply with UN resolutions.

Saddam was listening. Four days later, Iraq told the UN that it had decided to allow the return of the United Nations weapons inspectors without conditions and was ready to discuss practical arrangements. Hans Blix met Iraqi delegates for this purpose. There followed a period of intense negotiations culminating in the UN Security Council unanimously adopting Resolution 1441 on 8 November.

Resolution 1441 gave Iraq 'a final opportunity to comply with its disarmament obligations'. A few days later, Iraq accepted its terms unconditionally. Crucially, passage of this resolution was achieved only by deliberate ambiguity over a key issue: if Saddam failed to comply, could the US and the UK take military action against him *without* further authority from the Security Council?

As we shall see later, this was a central question in the debate over the legality of the invasion.

However, it is important to note here that this resolution did not in itself give any basis to go to war against Iraq: this could only be provided by the implicit 'revival' of Resolutions 678 and 687, which gave authority for the launch of the first Gulf War and set conditions for the ceasefire. Moreover, even if these were revived, they would give no authority to go to war to achieve regime change.

This presented a very troublesome ambiguity. Nevertheless the passage of Resolution 1441 was the apogee of success for Blair's policy. The British prime minister seemed to have forestalled the prospect of a unilateral US assault on Iraq. He had re-established a UN process backed by all the Security Council and all of the United States' allies.

Had he fallen under the proverbial bus at this point, Tony Blair might now be classed among the greatest international statesmen of modern times. He might be remembered as the man who had persuaded a reluctant President Clinton to make his humanitarian intervention in Kosovo, authorized a brilliant British raid to change the course of a civil war in Sierra Leone, and persuaded a bellicose George W. Bush to take the path of legality rather than going to war in Iraq.

Unfortunately, from this point nothing at all went to plan for Tony Blair.

WEAPONS INSPECTORS RETURN TO IRAQ

On 27 November 2002 something momentous happened. UN weapons inspectors entered Iraq. It was the first time they had been in the country since December 1998, when they had been withdrawn for their own safety because the US and the UK were about to mount Operation Desert Fox.

To the surprise (and perhaps disappointment) of many observers, the group of inspectors from the atomic energy agency and UNMOVIC met no obstruction from Saddam's regime. Inspectors were given access to every site they asked to visit and inspect: 'on no particular occasion were we denied access', the head of UNMOVIC Hans Blix told the Chilcot Inquiry on 27 July 2010.[57]

In the three months they were in Iraq, the weapons inspectors conducted more than 900 inspections at over 500 sites. They visited dozens of sites which were regarded by British and US

---

57 Dr Hans Blix, transcript of oral evidence to the Iraq Inquiry, 27 July 2010. However, Blix went on to say that he did not get that 'proactive co-operation' that he wanted, pp. 47–8.

intelligence as suspicious.[58] However, they did not find weapons of mass destruction in a single one of them.

The findings were not all in the Iraqi regime's favour. Hans Blix announced the discovery of illegally imported conventional arms, which enlisted a hasty promise of greater co-operation from the Iraqis. Part of this discovery was that Iraq had manufactured missiles with a range slightly greater than the permitted 150 kilometres and the inspectors set in motion a programme to destroy them.

On 27 January 2003 Hans Blix and Mohamed ElBaradei of the IAEA reported back to the UN. They told the Security Council of gaps in the information supplied by Iraq. They also told the Security Council that their work had been obstructed by the regime. However, Blix added that despite these gaps he was still unable to conclude that Saddam had any viable weapons of mass destruction.

On 14 February Blix again reported to the Security Council that he and his team had found no evidence of such weapons, adding that they had conducted some productive interviews with Saddam's scientists. This evidence undercut the dramatic presentation by Colin Powell just over a week earlier at the Security Council alleging evidence for Iraq's WMD. It also meant a headache for Tony Blair.

---

58   JIC member William Ehrman told the Foreign Affairs Select Committee that 'every single site' mentioned in the government's dossier on Iraq's weapons of mass destruction had been visited by UNMOVIC. Examination of Witnesses, Minutes of Evidence, 27 June 2003.

BLAIR FORCED TO CHOOSE

Ever since his meeting with George W. Bush at Crawford eleven months earlier, Tony Blair had been pursuing two parallel strategies.

On the one hand, the prime minister supported the United States in its desire for regime change. On the other hand, he was insistent that the war should be conducted on a legal basis through the United Nations.

These strategies did not need to be contradictory. Had Iraq refused to allow in the weapons inspectors, then UN Security Council authorization could have been obtained for an invasion. Had Iraq impeded the work of the inspectors after they arrived, the Security Council would probably have authorized invasion.

Alternatively the weapons inspectors might have discovered that Saddam Hussein did indeed have a secret project to create a stockpile of nuclear, chemical and biological weapons. Once again the existence of such a project could well have given grounds for invasion. Best of all (from the would-be invaders' point of view), the inspectors might have found actual possession of something which could be classed as lethal weaponry justifying war. Unfortunately for Tony Blair none of these outcomes applied. Saddam Hussein allowed the weapons inspectors into Iraq. Although not totally compliant or co-operative, Saddam allowed them to carry out their mission. When they set about their work they could find neither chemical or biological weapons (even when prompted by Western intelligence services) nor any evidence that Iraq had taken any steps to reconstitute its nuclear weapons programme.[59]

Tony Blair was therefore confronted with the dilemma that had haunted him and his advisers ever since Crawford. He had to choose between the United Nations and the United States, between legality and illegality, between peace and war.

The majority position of the UN Security Council was clear enough. Most members[60] wanted the weapons inspectors to continue their work until they were satisfied that Iraq was disarmed as required by Security Council resolutions, or until they reported to the Security Council that, because the Iraqi regime was obstructing their work, they were unable to come to a decision on this matter – in which case it should have been up to the Security Council to decide what further action needed to be taken.

French Foreign Minister Dominique de Villepin was an eloquent advocate for this view. Speaking to the Security Council on 14 February 2003, he said:

> Therefore, let us give the United Nations inspectors the time that
> is necessary for their mission to succeed. But let us together be
> vigilant and ask Mr. Blix and Mr. El-Baradei to report regularly
> to the Council ... Thus we would be able to judge the progress

---

59 Hans Blix told the Iraq Inquiry that he grew more sceptical about the intelligence concerning Saddam's weapons of mass destruction the longer his mission was in Iraq.

60 Those wanting the weapons inspectors to continue their work were Russia, France and China as permanent members of the Security Council together with temporary members Angola, Cameroon, Chile, Germany, Guinea, Mexico, Pakistan and Syria. Only Spain and Bulgaria supported the British and American position.

made and what remains to be accomplished. In that context, the use of force is not justified at this time. There is an alternative to war: disarming Iraq through inspections.

Moreover, premature recourse to the military option would be fraught with risks. The authority of our action rests today on the unity of the international community. Premature military intervention would call that unity into question, and that would remove its legitimacy and, in the long run, its effectiveness. Such intervention could have incalculable consequences for the stability of a scarred and fragile region. It would compound the sense of injustice, would aggravate tensions and would risk paving the way for other conflicts.[61]

Looked at in retrospect, this was an eerily prescient speech. De Villepin was applauded in the Security Council when he made it. It set out a course of action which would probably have led to a peaceful resolution of the Iraq crisis. By now the military timetable was far advanced. The US plan was to station some 200,000 US troops in the Gulf region, 55,000 of whom were in Kuwait, and to launch the air assault for the invasion during the 'moonless nights' at the end of February.[62] This date was now looming, and left small scope for the weapons inspectors to complete their work.

On 24 February Britain joined the United States and Spain in tabling a new UNSC resolution that stated 'Iraq has failed to take the final opportunity afforded to it in Resolution 1441.' The

61   Record of the 4707th meeting of the Security Council, S/PV.4707, p. 13.
       See http://www.un.org/en/ga/search/view_doc.asp?symbol=S/PV.4707.
62   See '10 Years Ago the US invaded Iraq', *US News and World Report*,
       19 March 2013.

following day Blair told the House of Commons that this resolution would not be put to a vote immediately: 'Instead, we will delay it to give Saddam one further final chance to disarm voluntarily.'[63]

By now, the Security Council was showing ever deeper public divisions over the need for military action, which Iraq exploited by publicly destroying a number of missiles.[64] On 7 March Hans Blix reported to the Security Council that Iraq had made progress on disarmament and was showing more co-operation with his inspectors.[65] This induced Blair to recast the proposed new resolution, to list six specific demands which Iraq had to fulfil by 17 March.[66]

The French, leading the group of states opposing the drive to war in 2003, promptly rejected this 17 March ultimatum. Unhelpfully for Blair, his attorney general at this point issued legal advice supporting the need for a further UN resolution to authorize war.

---

63   *Hansard*, House of Commons Debates, 25 February, 2003, Col 124.
64   During the first week of March Iraq destroyed over thirty of its stockpile of 100 al-Samoud 2 missiles, a development greeted by Blix as 'the most spectacular and the most important and tangible' example of real disarmament. 'Divided Security Council Awaits Blix's Assessment', *Independent*, 6 March 2003.
65   'Oral introduction of the twelfth quarterly report of UNMOVIC' to the Security Council by Dr Hans Blix, 7 March 2003, http://www.un.org/depts/unmovic/SC7asdelivered.htm.
66   The six 'benchmark' tests included: a public statement by Saddam Hussein, broadcast in Iraq, admitting possession of weapons of mass destruction, stating his regime has decided to give them up and pledging to co-operate with UN weapons inspectors; a commitment to allow Iraqi scientists to be interviewed by the inspectors outside Iraq; the surrender of, and explanation of the 10,000 litres of anthrax the Iraqis were believed to still be holding; a commitment to the destruction of proscribed missiles; an account of the unmanned aerial vehicles and remotely piloted vehicles or drones; and a commitment to surrender all mobile bio-production laboratories for destruction. As summarized in 'Straw Spells Out Key Tests for Saddam', *Guardian*, 12 March 2003.

THE AGONY OF LORD GOLDSMITH

All the evidence suggests that by now Tony Blair had decided that in the end he would ditch the United Nations route and join the United States in an attack on Iraq. But one huge obstacle needed to be overcome if the prime minister was to order British troops into battle. He had to show that the invasion was lawful.

This was not simply to persuade Labour MPs. Our generals needed to be quite certain that the mere presence of British troops in the battlefield did not constitute a war crime. Only one person in Britain could make the ruling that the war was legal. This was the attorney general, Lord Goldsmith.

Peter Goldsmith, an ambitious and gifted lawyer, had been created a life peer in 1999 and promoted to attorney general after the 2001 general election victory. Nothing in his life had prepared him for the responsibility he faced in the early spring of 2003. Thanks to circumstances he could never have foreseen, he had suddenly become one of the few people in Britain with the power to stop Tony Blair leading the country into war. He was a commercial barrister with no relevant political experience.

His deputy, Solicitor General Harriet Harman, was little help. She was trying to rebuild a political career in a junior position after being sacked as Blair's Social Security Secretary. She was not asked to give any evidence to the Chilcot Inquiry – nor was she once mentioned in other people's evidence, which suggests that she had no role in the intense debate over the legality of the war. Goldsmith faced this decision alone.

Goldsmith took a consistent view throughout 2002 that war

against Saddam would require some new authority from the United Nations. This was also the view of the Foreign Office's senior legal advisers, Sir Michael Wood and his deputy Elizabeth Wilmshurst. To Blair's frequent annoyance, Goldsmith volunteered this view, orally and in writing, at key moments. Blair consistently ignored all these warnings, on the curious grounds that he did not want to know whether or not war would be lawful until he was on the point of deciding whether or not to go to war.

In July 2002 Peter Goldsmith warned a meeting in Downing Street that there was no case for war against Saddam on grounds of self-defence (in response to actual or imminent attack) or on the emerging doctrine of humanitarian intervention. Knowing that Blair was about to meet Bush, he put this advice in writing on 30 July, warning him that war would require a fresh determination by the Security Council of 'material and flagrant breach' by Iraq of its obligations under extant resolutions – and that alone might not be sufficient. The Security Council might also have to give new authority to member states to use force in response to such a breach.[67]

In October Goldsmith met David Manning, Blair's foreign policy adviser, and Baroness Morgan, Blair's director of political and government relations. (Morgan would crop up again in the legal narrative. It is a reflection of Blair's style of government that at this

---

67 Goldsmith told the Chilcot Inquiry, in somewhat tortured language: 'I didn't want there to be any doubt that in my view the Prime Minister could not have the view that he could agree with President Bush somehow "Let's go without going back to the United Nations".' His advice was not terribly welcome, but he thought it might have helped Blair to decide to persuade Bush to follow the UN route. Transcript of Lord Goldsmith's evidence to the Chilcot Inquiry, 27 January 2010, p. 23.

point a 'special adviser' knew more about his attorney general's evolving advice than most cabinet ministers – and the Queen.)[68]

Goldsmith repeated his advice that force could not be used against Saddam without a fresh determination from the Security Council that he was in material breach of his obligations. He added that regime change was not a lawful reason for the use of force, which must be limited to what was necessary to make Saddam comply with UN resolutions.[69]

Remarkably, Peter Goldsmith was not asked to advise on the drafting of what would become UN Security Council Resolution 1441. He complained about this and warned Jack Straw that the drafts he had seen were not achieving the British/US objective of avoiding the need for a further resolution to authorize force against Saddam. Goldsmith met Blair on 22 October, before the adoption of 1441 when he again repeated that force against Saddam would require the authority of a new UN resolution.[70]

From this point, Goldsmith had to wrestle with the deliberate

---

68   In mid-2003 the Select Committee on Foreign Affairs questioned Alastair Campbell. John Maples MP was particularly concerned with 'issues of the machinery of government' in the run-up to the war and what he termed the 'informal *ad hoc* meetings' of figures who were 'political appointments in Downing Street'. Campbell stressed the meetings were neither informal nor *ad hoc*. Asked whether the Foreign Secretary was always present, Campbell replied: 'No is the answer to that because the Foreign Secretary does not work in Downing Street. I sit in an office and my phone goes regularly during the day, "Can you pop round and see the Prime Minister." He does not say, "Can you bring Jack Straw every time you come."' Maples answered: 'So there were meetings which the Prime Minister called at which his special advisers were present and his foreign policy adviser but no other minister?' Campbell replied: 'Absolutely, of course there were.' Minutes of Evidence, Examination of Witness (Questions 1100–19), 25 June 2003.

69   Transcript of Lord Goldsmith's evidence to the Chilcot Inquiry, 27 January 2010, pp. 25–6.

70   Ibid., pp. 26, 30–3.

ambiguity built into UNSCR 1441. No provision in this resolution would in itself authorize the use of force against Saddam. The issue was the relationship of 1441 to previous resolutions. Could 1441 establish that Saddam was in violation of UNSCR 687 (which established the ceasefire in the Gulf War of 1991), and thereby 'revive' the authorization to use force in UNSCR 678 (which called on member states to secure Iraqi withdrawal from Kuwait)? On such arcane issues, he had to decide on the legality of the war his prime minister wanted.

If Saddam were in breach of the conditions set out in 1441, could member states end the ceasefire and go back to war against him? Could they make this decision on their own, or would this require some form of further approval from the Security Council?

These were the key points which had been left deliberately ambiguous to secure passage of 1441. Goldsmith also had to examine the questions which needed answering in order to revive the right to resume hostilities against Saddam, namely: 1) is Iraq in breach of its obligations under UN resolutions (a question of fact), 2) is this a 'material' breach (a question of fact and judgement), and 3) is force a necessary and appropriate way to deal with such a breach (a question of judgement)? Could member states answer *all* of these questions for themselves or did they require some further deliberation by the Security Council?

Goldsmith yet again warned Blair on 30 January 2003 that Resolution 1441 'did not authorize the use of military force without a further determination of the Security Council'.[71]

---

71   Ibid., pp. 78–9, 90.

Blair was annoyed by this advice, and minuted that he did not understand it. His response was to dispatch Goldsmith to Washington, to meet some of the Bush administration's lawyers, who gave him more details of the negotiation of 1441. In particular they told him that the French had admitted that 1441 could 'automatically' authorize the use of force without further Security Council proceedings. It is striking that on this occasion Lord Goldsmith travelled to Washington to get their interpretation of 1441, but not it appears to Paris to get the French account. Goldsmith denies that he ever gave in to political pressure. Bush's lawyers also told him, as did Jack Straw, that they simply would never have accepted any resolution which did not allow for automatic authority to use force against Saddam.

For the first time, Goldsmith began to waver. On 12 February he sent Blair some new 'draft advice'. He warned Blair that UNSCR 1441 had not 'immediately' reactivated 678 and 687 and that 'the safest legal course would be to secure the adoption of a further Council decision' before using force against Saddam. However, for the first time, he said that there was a 'reasonable' case for going to war without a further resolution or decision by the Security Council.[72]

Goldsmith held this line in the advice he gave Blair on 7 March, which would be his last fully argued advice before the outbreak of war. Yes, there was a reasonable case for going to war without further authority from the Security Council. But it

---

72   http://www.iraqinquiry.org.uk/media/46490/Goldsmith-draft-advice-12February2003.pdf.

was far from certain that it would prevail in a court and again, the 'safer course' was to go back to the Security Council.[73]

With the intended war only days away, Blair asked Goldsmith to clarify this advice, as did the legal adviser to the Ministry of Defence (not, as is often claimed, the Chief of the Defence Staff Sir Michael Boyce). Goldsmith asked Blair for confirmation that Saddam was in material breach of Resolutions 678 and 687, to which Blair replied yes. Goldsmith did not ask Blair for any evidence of this view or any assessment of the seriousness of the breach, because Blair's simple confirmation was all he needed to get to the US position after all.

Goldsmith was now ready to say that in 2003 any Security Council member could determine as a matter of individual judgement that Saddam Hussein was in breach of two resolutions

---

73 Very significantly, on 7 March Goldsmith took aim at the US interpretation of 1441. He said: 'The UK has consistently taken the view … that, as the ceasefire conditions were set by the Security Council in resolution 687, it is for the Council to assess whether any such breach of those obligations has occurred. The US have a rather different view: they maintain that the fact of whether Iraq is in breach is a matter of objective fact which may therefore be assessed by individual member states. I am not aware of any other state which supports this view. This is an issue of critical importance when considering the effect of resolution 1441.' The US position would remove the Security Council from any role in answering questions 1), 2) and 3) set out above. Member states could answer each of them and proceed to use force if they gave themselves the right answer. Goldsmith gave three powerful reasons for rejecting that American view. First, it ignored the language of 1441 when it called for an 'assessment' by the Security Council of the seriousness of any breach by Iraq. Second, it ignored the reference in 1441 to 'international peace and security' and only the Security Council could determine whether this was under threat. Third, the US view would reduce the Security Council discussion to 'a procedural formality' and member states could go to war even if most Council members in the discussion were opposed to it. Goldsmith advice, 7 March 2003, paragraph 24 (i) … (iii). http://www.theguardian.com/politics/2005/apr/28/election2005.uk.

framed in the circumstances of 1990 and 1991 – and that was enough to allow them to start a new war even if all the other Security Council members were opposed to it.

This was the logical conclusion of the 'revival' argument, which Goldsmith had now adopted after his long resistance. Iraq is declared to be in material breach of its disarmament obligations under UNSCR 687 and subsequent resolutions. That 'revives' the status quo before the passage of 687, so that military action against Iraq, which stopped in April 1991, can now restart under the authority of UNSCR 678.

However, it is at least arguable that Goldsmith's new reasoning omitted one crucial final step. Even if UNSCR 678 had been 'revived' it never authorized the use of force to achieve regime change. Force would become lawful under 678 only if it was necessary and proportionate to the objectives of that resolution. These were the liberation of Kuwait and its subsequent protection – both objectives long achieved and not threatened by Saddam Hussein in 2003.

The other objective of 678 was the restoration of peace and security to the region of states in proximity to Iraq. Was this regional security threatened by Saddam in 2003, and threatened so badly as to require his removal? Goldsmith's final advice took no account of this point. It would have been hard to argue in the absence of evidence of WMD and with an abundance of evidence that Saddam's conventional forces were weak and ramshackle – and given that Saddam had no control over large tracts of his airspace.

Goldsmith communicated his helpfully revised view, based on the 'revival' argument, to the Ministry of Defence for the benefit of the service chiefs, and to Baroness Morgan and Lord Falconer for the benefit of Tony Blair. (It is sometimes alleged that they pressured Goldsmith to change his mind. He denied this strongly to the Chilcot Inquiry, and the timing of other records suggests that he had changed his mind already. But again, it is a fact that crucial legal advice was received by the Blair inner circle before it reached the full cabinet or the Queen.)

On 17 March the full cabinet heard from Goldsmith through a brief, unequivocal nine-paragraph statement, which unusually was made public through an arranged parliamentary question in the House of Lords. No one in the cabinet asked him a question about it – but then very few members were aware of his previous advice.

The last obstacle to war had been removed. Like Blair himself, when the attorney general was finally compelled to choose between the United Nations and the United States, he chose the United States. It was at this point that Elizabeth Wilmshurst, Deputy Legal Adviser at the Foreign Office, memorably resigned. Although not published at the time, her resignation letter stated: 'I cannot agree that it is lawful to use force against Iraq without a second Security Council Resolution to revive the authorization given in SCR 678'.[74] Although there were no other resignations from the Foreign Office, all twenty-seven members of the Foreign Office legal team agreed with her view that the war was unlawful.

---

74   See http://news.bbc.co.uk/1/hi/uk_politics/4377605.stm. Wilmshurst had been a Foreign Office lawyer since 1974 and served as (legal) counsellor in the UK mission to the United Nations in the late 1990s.

THE LAST DAYS OF PEACE

On 11 March the prime minister had been offered an unexpected get-out clause. Donald Rumsfeld in a press conference suddenly announced that because of Blair's domestic political problems, British forces could be excluded from the initial assault on Saddam. It was described as a 'Private Godfrey moment'[75] – at the last minute, Britain could be excused. The opportunity was not taken. Blair later claimed in his memoirs that Britain's military 'took amiss any sense that we might be in the second rank'.[76] Was that really the military opinion – or his own?

In spite of the French attitude to an ultimatum, confirmed on 14 March by a personal call from President Chirac, Blair continued to drum up support for his resolution. He hoped to secure the moral effect of nine Security Council votes in its favour even if the French (or Russians) vetoed it. Government ministers were sent scurrying around the world to each of the current Security Council members. Bush had given him only a one-week extension from the scheduled invasion on 10 March (forfeiting the advantage of the moonless nights).

On 17 March Blair gave up on his resolution. He met his cabinet and told them that Britain would join President Bush's invasion of Iraq, come what may. Robin Cook resigned. His statement denouncing a war 'without international authority or domestic support' electrified the House of Commons. Two junior ministers resigned with him: John Denham and Lord

---

75   By Graham Allen MP.
76   T. Blair, *A Journey*, Arrow, 2011, p. 433.

(Philip) Hunt. Both were a surprise: they had been loyal Blairites.

The following day the prime minister won the backing of the House of Commons. His emotional speech swayed many doubtful Labour MPs and spared him the danger of being opposed by the majority of his party. Labour opposition to Blair was ineptly led by Peter Kilfoyle, a former defence minister, and there was no effective challenge to a series of doubtful and misleading and false statements in Blair's speech.

FIVE

THE FAILURE
OF PARLIAMENT

---

*'The case against President Saddam's twelve-year
history of obstructing the United Nations' attempts at
disarmament has never been better made.'*

THE *INDEPENDENT* ON TONY BLAIR'S SPEECH TO THE
HOUSE OF COMMONS OF 18 MARCH 2003

On 18 March 2003 Tony Blair proposed a motion to the
House of Commons authorizing military action against Iraq.
Remarkably, the motion itself was misleading – and information
was readily available to MPs at the time to prove this. Nevertheless, the House of Commons passed the motion overwhelmingly
by 412 votes to 149.

Support from the Conservative opposition meant that the
result was not in doubt. However, there was real drama because

the prime minister faced a major revolt in his own party, along with ministerial resignations.

The prime minister's speech in proposing the motion was widely praised, and not just by supporters of the war. The *Independent*, which was against war, saluted Tony Blair the following day for delivering the 'most persuasive case yet by the man who has emerged as the most formidable persuader for war on either side of the Atlantic. The case against President Saddam's twelve-year history of obstructing the United Nations' attempts at disarmament has never been better made.'[77]

The motion claimed that President Chirac had said in a TV interview a week earlier on 10 March that France would always veto a Security Council resolution authorizing military action against Iraq. But this was an incomplete account of what M. Chirac said. In fact, the president merely restated the consistent French position that disarmament by inspection (which was proceeding more or less unhindered at that time) should continue until inspectors reported that disarmament by inspection was impossible. Then, and only then, should the Security Council consider authorizing military action to disarm Iraq. In that case, 'regrettably, the war would become inevitable', he said, but 'it isn't today'.

The House of Commons failed lamentably to scrutinize the government's case for war effectively on 18 March 2003. Not only did MPs fail to expose Tony Blair's account of what President Chirac had said, they failed also to challenge him on other misleading

---

77 'Leading Article – Whatever the Anxieties Over This Conflict, Mr Blair Has Shown Himself to be a Leader', *Independent*, 19 March 2003.

assertions and omissions, when information was in the public domain to enable them to do so. For example:

- his misleading assertion that pre-Gulf War chemical and biological agents deemed 'unaccounted for' by UN inspectors actually existed;
- his failure to tell the House of Commons that even if these agents did exist many of them would have degraded by then and would no longer be useful as warfare agents;
- his failure to tell the House of Commons that Saddam Hussein's son-in-law told UN inspectors in 1995 that, on his orders, all Iraq's proscribed weapons had been destroyed.

THE TRUTH BEHIND FRANCE'S 'VETO'

Tony Blair's claim that President Chirac said France would always veto military action was incorporated into the government motion passed by the House of Commons. The motion stated:

> That this House ... regrets that despite sustained diplomatic effort by Her Majesty's Government it has not proved possible to secure a second Resolution in the UN because one Permanent Member of the Security Council made plain in public its intention to use its veto whatever the circumstances.

In his speech Tony Blair removed all ambiguity by identifying the offending permanent member as France: 'Last Monday, we were getting very close with it [the second resolution]. We very nearly had the majority agreement ... Yes, there were debates about the length of the ultimatum, but the basic construct was gathering support. Then, on Monday night, France said that it would veto a second resolution, whatever the circumstances.'[78]

This account was selective. Tony Blair did not tell MPs that President Chirac had made it very clear in the interview on that Monday night that there were indeed circumstances in which France would *not* veto a resolution for war.[79]

Chirac identified two different scenarios: one in which the UN inspectors reported progress, and the other where the inspectors reported that their task was impossible – in which case, in his words, 'regrettably, the war would become inevitable'. That portion reads:

> The inspectors have to tell us: 'we can continue and, at the end of a period which we think should be of a few months' – I'm saying a few months because that's what they have said – 'we shall have completed our work and Iraq will be disarmed'. Or they will come and tell the Security Council: 'we are sorry but Iraq isn't cooperating, the progress isn't sufficient, we aren't in a position to achieve our goal, we won't be able to guarantee Iraq's disarmament'. In that case it will be for the Security

---

78 *Hansard*, House of Commons Debates, 18 March 2003, cols 760–4.
79 Translated excerpts of TV interview by President Chirac to TF1 and France2, 10 March 2003, www.david-morrison.org.uk/other-documents/chirac-20030310.htm. A French transcript of the full interview is accessible here: http://www.jacqueschirac-asso.fr/fr/wp-content/uploads/2010/04/ITW-IRAK-10_03_2003.pdf.

Council and it alone to decide the right thing to do. But in that case, of course, regrettably, the war would become inevitable. It isn't today.

From that, it is clear that there were circumstances in which France would *not* have vetoed military action, namely, if the UN inspectors reported that they couldn't do their job. But, he made clear, since disarmament by inspection was still possible, at this time France would vote 'no' to any resolution giving a green light to war.[80]

There is evidence that Tony Blair had not simply made a mistake. After Chirac's interview, Blair took a deliberate decision to blame France for the failure of the United States and Britain to persuade more than two other members of the Security Council (Spain and Bulgaria) to vote for the second resolution.

This was confirmed in evidence to the Chilcot Inquiry on

---

80 Clare Short, a cabinet colleague of the prime minister in March 2003, later accused Tony Blair of misleading Parliament over President Chirac's position. On 4 June 2003, she raised the issue with him in the Commons, asking 'did the Prime Minister apologise to President Chirac for misleading all of us about the position of France on the second resolution? I think that he told the House, and many of us, that France had said that it would veto any second resolution. It is now absolutely clear that President Chirac said on 10 March that the inspectors needed longer, but if they failed to disarm Iraq, the Security Council would have to mandate military action. Does that not mean that he misled us and should apologise to us as well?' In his response Blair again emphasised that Chirac's remarks 'were about France saying no whatever the circumstances', before detailing that 'France made it clear that it would not accept any resolution that involved the automatic use of force in the absence of compliance by Saddam or an ultimatum ... Therefore, we would have been back in a situation in which we would have had to come back to the Security Council once again and come to another resolution, but without any threat to use force if Saddam did not comply.' *Hansard*, House of Commons Debates, 4 June 2003, cols 166–7.

10 September 2010 by Matthew Rycroft, who was Tony Blair's private secretary (foreign affairs). Rycroft was asked, 'Was there a conscious decision for reasons of domestic political presentation to pin the blame on the French when, in fact, the situation was that we had failed to get the Chileans and the Mexicans across [to vote for the second resolution] and had no prospect at this stage actually of getting our resolution?' He replied, 'Yes.'[81] This account of events was substantiated by Sir Stephen Wall, who was Tony Blair's European Union adviser from 2000 to 2004. He reported in evidence to the Chilcot Inquiry that on the day after the Chirac interview he had witnessed Tony Blair in a Downing Street corridor give Alastair Campbell 'his marching orders to play the anti-French card with the *Sun* and others'.[82]

So it was clear that Tony Blair was not candid to the House of Commons on 18 March 2003 about the real attitude of France to taking military action against Iraq.[83]

---

81 Matthew Rycroft in private session before Iraq Inquiry, 10 September 2010. See www.iraqinquiry.org.uk/media/50560/20100910-Rycroft.pdf.

82 www.iraqinquiry.org.uk/media/51760/20110119-wall-final.pdf, p.68. Sir Stephen Wall gave a fuller account of this incident when interviewed by the author for *Peter Oborne's Chilcot Report* on Radio 4 on 29 October 2015: 'I was walking down the corridor with Tony Blair and Alastair Campbell and they were saying to each other that they would brief in a particular brief to the *Sun* that Chirac had made it clear that in no circumstances was he prepared to go to war against Saddam Hussein. And Alastair Campbell duly briefed, and I think it was out on the radio because I had a phone call from … from Joyce Quin, Labour MP, and she said to me "I … Stephen, I've just heard on the radio what No. 10 are saying about Chirac, but you know does the prime minister realize that isn't actually what Chirac said?" And I said, "Joyce, I think he does realize very well that that's not what Chirac actually said".'

   The author responded: 'That's amazing. So what you're saying there is that Downing Street deliberately lied about Chirac's statement?' Stephen Wall replied: 'Yes.'

83 Only one MP – Labour's Lynne Jones – raised this issue in the debate. She intervened in a speech by Michael Ancram, Conservative foreign affairs

THE TRUTH ABOUT 'UNACCOUNTED FOR' PRE-GULF WAR CHEMICAL AND BIOLOGICAL AGENTS

On 6 March 2003 UNMOVIC, the UN weapons inspectorate, published a 173-page document entitled *Unresolved Disarmament Issues: Iraq's Proscribed Weapons Programmes*.[84] This originated as an internal working document prepared by UNMOVIC identifying the 'key remaining disarmament tasks' that Iraq had to complete.

The document contained a comprehensive survey of Iraq's chemical and biological weapons programmes and the subsequent use or destruction of weapons and weapons-related material, based on information assembled by UN inspectors from 1991 onwards. It ended with an assessment of unresolved issues for each agent and weapon, and a statement of what Iraq needs to do to resolve them.

In the days prior to the invasion of Iraq, Tony Blair and his foreign secretary, Jack Straw, used this document shamelessly, giving the impression that it contained new and damning evidence that Iraq possessed proscribed weapons.[85] In reality, it contained

---

spokesman, and quoted what Chirac said. But she was treated with contempt by Ancram, who dismissed her as 'an apologist for the French president'. *Hansard*, House of Commons Debates, 18 March 2003, Col 891.

84 http://www.un.org/depts/unmovic/documents/UNMOVIC%20UDI%20 Working%20Document%206%20March%202003.pdf.

85 Jack Straw told the Commons: 'The full extent of that iceberg [Iraq's illegal weapons programme] was revealed in a document compiled by UNMOVIC entitled "Unresolved Disarmament Issues: Iraq's Proscribed Weapons Programmes", which was made publicly available late on 7 March. I have also placed copies of that document in the Library. I commend it to all Members. It sets out, in 173 pages of painstaking detail, the terrible nature of the weapons that Saddam has sought with such determination to develop. It is a chilling catalogue of evasion, deceit and feigning co-operation while in reality pursuing concealment. The sheer scale of Iraq's efforts to develop

NOT THE CHILCOT REPORT

little or nothing new: it did not claim that Iraq possessed banned weapons or weapons-related material, merely that certain material was 'unaccounted for'.

Nor did it suggest that Iraq had any operational agent or weapon production facilities. And it confirmed that many of the agents manufactured before the Gulf War would have degraded by then and would no longer be useful in war.

In his speech in the House of Commons on 18 March 2003 the prime minister, nonetheless, described the UNMOVIC report as a 'remarkable document', and quoted from it, for example, on mustard gas:

> Mustard constituted an important part ... of Iraq's CW [chemical weapons] arsenal ... 550 mustard filled shells and up to 450 mustard filled aerial bombs unaccounted for.

These words can indeed be found on page 76 of the document, but crucially they do not give the sense of the text from which they were extracted. That text is as follows (with his extract underlined):

> Judging by the quantities produced, weaponized and used, <u>Mustard constituted an important part</u> (about 70%) <u>of Iraq's CW arsenal</u>.
>
> There is much evidence, including documents provided by Iraq and information collected by UNSCOM, to suggest that

those weapons and to hide them can be grasped only by reading the whole document, as I have done.' *Hansard*, House of Commons Debates, 10 March 2003, Col 21.

most quantities of mustard remaining in 1991, as declared by Iraq, were destroyed under UNSCOM supervision. The remaining gaps are related to the accounting for mustard filled aerial bombs and artillery projectiles. There are <u>550 mustard filled shells and up to 450 mustard filled aerial bombs unaccounted for since 1998</u>. The mustard filled shells account for a couple of tonnes of agent while the aerial bombs account for approximately 70 tonnes. According to an investigation made by the Iraqi 'Depot Inspection Commission', the results of which were reported to UNMOVIC in March 2003, the discrepancy in the accounting for the mustard filled shells could be explained by the fact that Iraq had based its accounting on approximations.

In other words these shells containing mustard gas (a crude chemical agent of First World War vintage) may never have existed. The prime minister's other extracts from the document are also misleading. Tony Blair told the House of Commons that day:

When the inspectors left in 1998, they left unaccounted for 10,000 litres of anthrax; a far-reaching VX nerve agent programme; up to 6,500 chemical munitions; at least 80 tonnes of mustard gas, and possibly more than 10 times that amount; unquantifiable amounts of sarin, botulinum toxin and a host of other biological poisons; and an entire Scud missile programme. We are asked now seriously to accept that in the last few years – contrary to all history, contrary to all intelligence – Saddam

decided unilaterally to destroy those weapons. I say that such
a claim is palpably absurd.

So we can see here that Blair stated as a fact that proscribed
material deemed 'unaccounted for' by UN inspectors actually
existed. In doing so, he seriously misled the House of Commons.[86]

This egregious misrepresentation was compounded by the fact
he did not mention that the UNMOVIC document made it clear
that, though the anthrax may still exist, any 'unaccounted for'
sarin, VX and botulinum toxin would have degraded and would
no longer be effective as warfare agents:

> There is no evidence that any bulk Sarin-type agents remain in
> Iraq – gaps in accounting of these agents are related to Sarin-
> type agents weaponized in rocket warheads and aerial bombs.
> Based on the documentation found by UNSCOM during inspec-
> tions in Iraq, Sarin-type agents produced by Iraq were largely
> of low quality and as such, degraded shortly after production.
> Therefore, with respect to the unaccounted for weaponized Sarin-
> type agents, it is unlikely that they would still be viable today.[87]

---

86 Hans Blix told the author that 'when Mr Blair asserts that there were weapons, well that's an assertion and it was not supported by evidence. Both the
UK and the US replaced question marks by exclamation marks. I certainly
think it was a misrepresentation.' See 'We don't need to wait for Chilcot, Blair
lied to us about Iraq. Here's the evidence', openDemocracy, 28 October 2005.
https://www.opendemocracy.net/uk/peter-oborne/we-dont-need-to-wait-
for-chilcot-we-were-lied-to-heres-evidence.

87 UNMOVIC, *Unresolved Disarmament Issues: Iraq's Proscribed Weapons
Programmes*, 2003, p. 73. The UNMOVIC document also stated that 'VX
produced through route B [the method used by Iraq in 1990] must be used
relatively quickly after production (about 1 to 8 weeks), which would probably be satisfactory for wartime requirements' (p. 82). It added that 'any

Without that vital explanatory information, the prime minister's list of 'unaccounted for' warfare agents was hopelessly misleading.

THE TRUTH ABOUT HUSSEIN KAMAL'S INTELLIGENCE

Saddam Hussein's son-in-law Hussein Kamal was the director of Iraq's Military Industrialization Corporation, which was responsible for Iraq's chemical and biological weapons programmes. In summer 1995, he defected to Jordan and was interviewed by international weapons inspectors in Amman on 22 August. He later returned to Iraq and was executed. As a result of his defection, UNSCOM's knowledge of Iraq's biological weapons programme was greatly enhanced.

In the months before the US/UK invasion of Iraq, the British government continually cited Kamal as a valuable source of information about Iraq's weapons programmes, and as proof that interrogation of Iraqis who participated in these programmes, rather than detective work by UN inspectors, was the way to acquire a comprehensive picture of them.

Tony Blair returned to this theme on 18 March 2003:

> In August [1995], [Iraq] provided yet another full and final decla-
> ration. Then, a week later, Saddam's son-in-law, Hussein Kamal,

---

botulinum toxin that was produced and stored according to the methods described by Iraq and in the time period declared is unlikely to retain much, if any, of its potency. Therefore, any such stockpiles of botulinum toxin, whether in bulk storage or in weapons that remained in 1991, would not be active today' (ibid., p. 101).

defected to Jordan. He disclosed a far more extensive biological weapons programme and, for the first time, said that Iraq had weaponized the programme – something that Saddam had always strenuously denied.

Tony Blair did not divulge to Parliament that Kamal had also told UN inspectors that, on his orders, all Iraq's proscribed weapons had been destroyed. If he knew of this, it raises the question why he did not tell MPs.

Kamal was interviewed by Brent Sadler of CNN in September 1995. A transcript of that interview can still be read on the CNN website (at the time of writing). In it, Kamal states: 'Iraq does not possess any weapons of mass destruction.'[88]

LURCH TO WAR

Ultimately, Blair had put Bush's chosen timetable ahead of the time needed for the UN inspectors. At no point in his speech was he able to suggest that Britain or any other country would be in danger if they were given more time.

---

88   See edition.cnn.com/WORLD/9509/iraq_defector/kamel_transcript/index.html.
      Kamal had been interviewed in Amman on 22 August 1995 by the joint IAEA/UNSCOM team. A 'note for the file' on this interview can be read at www.casi.org.uk/info/unscom950822.pdf. In the note, Kamal is quoted as saying: 'I ordered destruction [sic] of all chemical weapons. All weapons – biological, chemical, missile, nuclear were destroyed' (p. 13). Lynne Jones was the only MP to point out that Hussein Kamal had said that 'Saddam Hussein destroyed all his stocks of chemical and biological weapons before 1993'. Yet again her information was dismissed with contempt. *Hansard*, House of Commons Debates, 18 March 2003, Col 860.

The motion before the House of Commons declared that Britain was taking military action to uphold the authority of the UN by disarming Iraq as required by Security Council resolutions:

> That this House ... believes that the United Kingdom must uphold the authority of the United Nations as set out in Resolution 1441 and many Resolutions preceding it, and therefore supports the decision of Her Majesty's Government that the United Kingdom should use all means necessary to ensure the disarmament of Iraq's weapons of mass destruction.

In his speech, Tony Blair asserted that the UN would lose all credibility if its disarmament resolutions against Iraq were not enforced:

> To will the ends but not the means would do more damage in the long term to the UN than any other single course that we could pursue. To fall back into the lassitude of the past twelve years, to talk, to discuss, to debate but never to act ... that is the worst course imaginable.

Upholding the authority of the Security Council sounds like a worthy objective, until you remember that in mid-March 2003 the Security Council was, by eleven to four, opposed to military action to enforce its disarmament resolutions against Iraq. The United States and Britain took it upon themselves to enforce the will of the Security Council – by overriding the will of the Security Council.

On 19 March the US launched a bombing raid targeted personally at Saddam Hussein. It was unsuccessful. The next day they opened an overwhelming 'shock-and-awe' offensive by air and land against Saddam's inferior and reluctant army.

As the bombs fell on the regime's demoralized troops, US and British military forces crossed the border from Kuwait into Iraq. The campaign to overthrow Saddam Hussein's regime by force had begun, without authority from the Security Council.

ENDGAME: UN INSPECTORS LEAVE IRAQ

On 18 March 2003, the same day Tony Blair was persuading MPs to vote for war, the UN inspectors were once again withdrawn from Iraq for their own safety.

The date for the military onslaught was not determined by the progress or otherwise of the ongoing weapons inspections. It was not triggered by the inspectors reporting that they couldn't do any more useful work. On the contrary, the inspectors were anxious to have more time to complete their mission.

The date, in reality, was determined only by the US military timetable, to which the UK had assented. The Bush administration decided that the US forces already massed in the region could not be held back any longer. The UK had already asked the US for a week's delay, which had been granted. A factor in refusing a further delay was the reluctance on the part of the US army to fight a war during the searingly hot Iraqi summer.

So, on 19 March 2003, the possibility of peaceful disarmament by inspection was aborted by the US and Britain without the consent of the Security Council. They, and they alone, made the decision to terminate disarmament by inspection, which was proceeding relatively unhindered, and to replace it by forceful military disarmament and regime change.

SIX

WAS THE INVASION LAWFUL?

'The US have a rather different view: they maintain
that the assessment of a breach is for individual
member States. We are not aware of any other
State which supports this view.'

FOREIGN & COMMONWEALTH OFFICE
LEGAL DOCUMENT, MARCH 2002[89]

I n Chapter 5 we detailed how Tony Blair, misrepresented and
falsified the facts in order to make the case for war.

We now ask the question: was the war lawful in any sense
at all? This requires going over some of the ground we covered
when describing the agonies of Lord Goldsmith in Chapter 4.

---

89   http://www.david-morrison.org.uk/other-documents/fcolegal020308.pdf.

But first of all: a reminder of first principles. It is a fundamental principle of international law that states are prohibited from using force except in self-defence[90] or unless its use is formally authorized by the Security Council under Chapter VII of the UN Charter. The Security Council authorized the use of force against Iraq twice:

1. in Resolution 678 passed in November 1990 to expel Iraq from Kuwait; and
2. in Resolution 687, the first disarmament resolution, passed in April 1991 (after Iraq had been expelled from Kuwait) to expel Iraq from Kuwait if it re-entered the country.

But the Security Council never authorized the use of force specifically to rid Iraq of 'weapons of mass destruction', but only to restore regional peace and security. It would be a hell of a stretch to assert that Britain was acting in self-defence against Iraqi aggression when it invaded Iraq alongside the United States in March 2003, and none of Iraq's neighbours saw it as an imminent threat. It would therefore appear that Britain had no grounds under UNSC 678 and 687 to take part in the invasion of Iraq. Therefore Britain's action was in breach of international law.

---

90 A number of recent military actions, particularly Kosovo in 1999, have been justified by their perpetrators under the newly-invented doctrine of 'humanitarian intervention'. This has yet to be established or even defined in international law. It was *not* a justification for the invasion of Iraq, as Goldsmith advised in July 2002: Goldsmith transcript of evidence to Iraq Inquiry, 27 January 2010, p. 21.

Although Britain maintained that Saddam Hussein was in breach of his obligations under the UN resolutions it never completed the further necessary step of establishing that Saddam Hussein's regime was a threat to regional peace and security, which could be eliminated *only* by his forcible removal.

It would therefore appear that Britain and the United States had no grounds under international law for the invasion of Iraq.

However, the legal advice given by the attorney general, Lord Goldsmith, on 17 March 2003 was that 'the authority to use force under resolution 678 has revived and so continues today'.[91]

In other words, a resolution passed in November 1990 to authorize military action to expel Iraq from Kuwait was said by the attorney general to authorize military action for an entirely different purpose in March 2003.

On the face of it, that is absurd, particularly when it is recalled that at most four of the fifteen members of the Security Council were in favour of such military action in March 2003.

THE ATTORNEY GENERAL'S LEGAL ADVICE

In early March 2003, before Britain and the US finally abandoned their quest for a 'second' Security Council resolution, the prime minister asked the attorney general to supply him with 'advice on the legality of military action' in the absence of such a resolution.

---

91   www.publications.parliament.uk/pa/ld200203/ldhansrd/vo030317/text/
30317wo1.htm.

This advice was contained in a thirteen-page document by the attorney general dated 7 March 2003.[92]

Lord Goldsmith's advice was equivocal about whether military action was lawful, merely saying that 'a reasonable case can be made' for it, but the attorney general stated this position unequivocally ten days later in a written answer in the House of Lords on 17 March 2003.

There has been controversy about the content of this advice, and how the caveats in it were absent from his final view of 17 March 2003. But little attention has been paid to the most important part of the advice of 7 March 2003, which is contained in the section entitled 'Possible consequences of acting without a second resolution' (paragraphs 32–5).

This section addressed the question that every client needs to have his lawyer answer, namely, what are the chances of me being convicted if I do what I'm thinking of doing? In this instance, would the UK be convicted of aggression, if military action is taken against Iraq? And further, would the prime minister himself face a trial for 'the planning, preparation, initiation or waging of a war of aggression', as Hermann Goering had done at Nuremberg? The attorney general's answers were: there's very little chance of it. In summary, he advised:

- Prosecution of the UK by the International Court of Justice (ICJ) was very unlikely.
- Prosecution of the prime minister by the International

Criminal Court (ICC) was impossible – the Rome Statute didn't include a crime of aggression at that time.

- Intervention by domestic courts to stop military action was very unlikely – the courts had already rejected a bid by CND to stop it.

The attorney general didn't have to state the most important fact of all, which is that, as a veto-wielding permanent member of the Security Council, the UK can take any military action it likes without fear of the mildest censure from the council, let alone economic or military sanctions being imposed to make it halt its military action.

With that, the attorney general assured Tony Blair that it was virtually certain that neither he nor the UK would be subject to legal action if the UK took military action against Iraq. In other words, taking military action would almost certainly be cost-free in legal terms for him and for the UK.[93]

This was true even if the attorney general had declared that military action against Iraq was not authorized by the Security Council, since even then there was no possibility of him or the UK being subject to legal action.

Having said that, the attorney general's decision was of immense *political* importance. Had he asserted that the proposed military action was not authorized by the Security Council,

---

93   It is conceivable that Blair might face charges of manslaughter under UK law for causing the deaths of British service personnel and Iraqi civilians in an unlawful war. The courts would have to decide whether he had had a duty of care towards these victims, and whether Blair's conduct fell so far below the standards of his position as to constitute gross negligence.

it is probable that Tony Blair would have had to call off British participation in the invasion. In written evidence to the Chilcot Inquiry in January 2011, Tony Blair wrote:

> Had Peter Goldsmith not finally been of the view when he came to give his formal advice that 1441 did authorize force, then the UK could not and would not have participated in the decision to remove Saddam.[94]

No doubt, the US would have continued with the invasion and overthrown Saddam Hussein's regime – the 150,000 US troops assembled in Kuwait for the invasion were not going to go home leaving Saddam Hussein in power – but international support for the US action would have been seriously undermined by the judgement that, according to their former partner in the enterprise, the US action was 'illegal'.

So a great deal hung on the attorney general's assertion that a Security Council resolution passed in November 1990 to authorize military action to expel Iraq from Kuwait also authorized military action to disarm Iraq in March 2003.

It is now necessary to examine his 'revival' argument in some depth. Contrary to Blair's statement immediately above, UNSCR 1441 did not not provide any authority for the use of force. What it achieved was to set out possible conditions to revive the authority for force under previous resolutions. But which resolutions were in fact revived?

---

94 'Tony Blair's Statement to the Iraq Inquiry', http://www.iraqinquiry.org.uk/media/50743/Blair-statement.pdf, p. 11.

COULD 678 BE REVIVED?

The essence of the attorney general's argument was that the authorization to use force in Security Council Resolution 678 passed in November 1990 to expel Iraq from Kuwait could be 'revived' if Iraq was in breach of its disarmament obligations under Security Council resolutions.

This argument was not new: it had been used before by the UK to claim Security Council authority for military action against Iraq at a time when the council was actually opposed to military action, for example, to assert that Operation Desert Fox – the US/UK bombing of Iraq in December 1998 – was in fact authorized by the Security Council.[95]

---

95 The basic argument, set out in a leaked FCO document, 'Iraq: Legal Background', from March 2002, is as follows:

Following its invasion and annexation of Kuwait, the Security Council authorized the use of force in Resolution 678 (1990); this resolution authorized coalition forces to use all necessary means to force Iraq to withdraw, and to restore international peace and security in the area. This resolution gave a legal basis for Operation Desert Storm, which was brought to an end by the cease-fire set out by the Council in Resolution 687 (1991). The conditions for the cease-fire in that resolution (and subsequent resolutions) imposed obligations on Iraq with regard to the elimination of WMD and monitoring of its obligations. Resolution 687 (1991) suspended but did not terminate the authority to use force in Resolution 678 (1990).

In the UK's view a violation of Iraq's obligations which undermines the basis of the cease-fire in Resolution 687 (1991) can revive the authorization to use force in Resolution 678 (1990). As the cease-fire was proclaimed by the Council in Resolution 687 (1991), it is for the Council to assess whether any such breach of those obligations has occurred. The US have a rather different view: they maintain that the assessment of a breach is for individual member States. We are not aware of any other State which supports this view.

The authorization of the use of force contained in Resolution 678 (1990) has been revived in this way on certain occasions. For example, when Iraq refused to cooperate with the UN Special Commission (UNSCOM) in 1997/8, a series of SCRs [Security Council resolutions] condemned the decision as unacceptable. In 1205 (1998) the Council condemned Iraq's decision to end

Unfortunately, the argument fails – because 678 could not be revived. It was superseded by the passage of UNSCR 687.

If, as the Foreign Office document above contends, 687 was a ceasefire resolution that suspended, but did not terminate, the authority to use force in 678, there would have been no need to include a further authority to use force in 687.

The inclusion of this new authority is a proof positive that the Security Council did not consider that the authority in 678 was merely suspended, and would revive if Iraq violated the ceasefire conditions by, for example, re-entering Kuwait.

In fact, 687 brought about a *permanent* ceasefire and terminated the authority to use force in 678. This is clear from examining 687 in conjunction with Resolution 686, passed a month earlier in March 1991. Resolution 686 established a provisional ceasefire, but in paragraph four explicitly states that the authorization for the use of force in 678 remains in effect. No similar provision is present in 687. Instead, 687 itself established new grounds for the use of force against Iraq – if it re-entered Kuwait or if it threatened regional peace and security. Moreover, 687 did not hand to member states the right to use force unilaterally. Its crucial paragraph, thirty-four, stated that the Security

---

all cooperation with UNSCOM as a flagrant violation of Iraq's obligations under 687 (1991), and restated that the effective operation of UNSCOM was essential for the implementation of the resolution. In our view these resolutions had the effect of causing authorization to use force to revive, which provided the legal basis for Operation Desert Fox.

See http://www.david-morrison.org.uk/other-documents/fcolegal020308. pdf. For the text of Resolution 1205 see http://www.un.org/en/ga/search/view_doc.asp?symbol=S/RES/1205%281998%29.

Council '[d]ecides to remain seized of the matter and to take such further steps as may be required for the implementation of the present resolution and to secure peace and security in the area'.[96]

BACK TO THE REVIVAL ARGUMENT

In the spring of 2002, the British government decided that it would be best to take the matter back to the Security Council and seek more explicit authority. By September 2002, the US had agreed to this course of action. Resolution 1441 was passed unanimously in November 2002, but one must emphasize yet again it did *not* provide explicit authority to use force, even if Iraq refused to admit inspectors.

At this point, the government abandoned hope of explicit authorization in a new resolution and accepted that it would have to fall back on the revival argument. To revive the authority to use force, a declaration was required by the Security Council that Iraq was in breach of its disarmament obligations. But on this point, 1441 was expressed in terms that precluded an instant resort to war against Iraq. On the one hand, in paragraph one it asserted that:

> Iraq has been and remains in material breach of its obligations under relevant resolutions, including resolution 687 (1991).

But, on the other hand, in paragraph two it gave Iraq:

---

96   http://www.un.org/Depts/unmovic/documents/687.pdf.

> A final opportunity to comply with its disarmament obligations
> under relevant resolutions of the Council.

So 1441 could hardly be taken as an immediate trigger for the revival of 678 authority for military action. Furthermore, paragraph four stated that:

> False statements or omissions in the declarations submitted by
> Iraq pursuant to this resolution and failure by Iraq at any time
> to comply with, and cooperate fully in the implementation of,
> this resolution shall constitute a further material breach of Iraq's
> obligations and will be reported to the Council for assessment
> in accordance with paragraphs 11 and 12 below.

This gave the definite impression that it was up to the Security Council to decide what should be done after 'assessment' by it of any non-compliance by Iraq reported to it.

THE SECOND RESOLUTION

Because of this, the UK set out to get the Security Council to adopt a second resolution with one operative paragraph, which said:

> [The Security Council] decides that Iraq has failed to take the
> final opportunity afforded to it by resolution 1441 (2002).[97]

---

97   See http://news.sky.com/story/169346/uk-us-and-spains-draft-resolution.

If that had been passed, the Security Council would have said, in effect, that Iraq was still in breach of its disarmament obligations – since it had failed to take the opportunity provided by 1441 to fulfil its disarmament obligations.

But, only four out of the fifteen members of the Security Council supported this resolution, even though it didn't explicitly authorize military action. At the time, of course, it was assumed that its passage would have given a Security Council green light to military action, and certainly the UK would have used it to assert that authority for military action had been revived.

However, despite President Bush twisting arms and threatening (and bugging the UN offices of recalcitrant members),[98] the Security Council refused to endorse the 'second' resolution. So, the attorney general was forced to modify the standard British version of the revival argument, set out in the Foreign Office document quoted above – instead of the Security Council being required to declare in a resolution that Iraq was in breach of its disarmament obligations, he adopted the United States position that it was sufficient for any individual member state of the UN, for example, the UK, to make such a declaration.

THE ATTORNEY GENERAL'S ANSWER

This brings us to the attorney general's written answer of 17 March 2003. The first three paragraphs are about the revival

---

98 'Revealed: US Dirty Tricks to Win Vote on Iraq War', *Observer*, 2 March 2003.

of 678 authority to take military action. As we have seen, 678 could not be revived: it was superseded by 687. However, the next three give an accurate summary of the effect of 1441 – and refer correctly to 687:

4. In resolution 1441 the Security Council determined that Iraq has been and remains in material breach of resolution 687, because it has not fully complied with its obligations to disarm under that resolution.

5. The Security Council in resolution 1441 gave Iraq 'a final opportunity to comply with its disarmament obligations' and warned Iraq of the 'serious consequences' if it did not.

6. The Security Council also decided in resolution 1441 that, if Iraq failed at any time to comply with and cooperate fully in the implementation of resolution 1441, that would constitute a further material breach.

The seventh and eighth are the ones that matter:

7. It is plain that Iraq has failed so to comply and therefore Iraq was at the time of resolution 1441 and continues to be in material breach.

8. Thus, the authority to use force under resolution 678 has revived and so continues today.[99]

---

99   http://www.publications.parliament.uk/pa/ld200203/ldhansrd/vo030317/text/30317w01.htm.

PRIME MINISTER CERTIFIES

The Butler Review published in July 2004 revealed that paragraph seven was the product of an exchange of letters between the attorney general and Tony Blair (in his capacity as the prime minister of the UK). Remarkably, the bare word of Tony Blair was the sole arbiter of fact for the attorney general to conclude that military action against Iraq was authorized by the Security Council.

As explained in the Butler Review (paragraphs 383–5), the attorney general wrote formally to Tony Blair on 14 March 2003 seeking confirmation that:

> It is unequivocally the Prime Minister's view that Iraq has committed further material breaches as specified in paragraph 4 of resolution 1441.

The prime minister replied the next day, saying:

> It is indeed the Prime Minister's unequivocal view that Iraq is in further material breach of its obligations, as in OP4 [Operative Paragraph 4] of UNSCR 1441, because of 'false statements or omissions in the declarations submitted by Iraq pursuant to this resolution and failure by Iraq to comply with, and co-operate fully in the implementation of, this resolution'.

The attorney general did not look behind the prime minister's 'unequivocal view'. He allowed Tony Blair to be the sole judge of the facts.

Blair's reply was enough for the attorney general to assert that the authority to take military action against Iraq, originally given in November 1990 to expel Iraq from Kuwait, was revived and that the upcoming invasion by the United States and the United Kingdom was authorized by the Security Council.

This reasoning could have applied equally to any other state which wanted to take military action against Iraq at any time since 1991. For example, Iran could have claimed authority from the Security Council to invade Iraq once the council had certified that Iraq was in breach of its disarmament obligations.

Lord Goldsmith's efforts to prove that UK military action against Iraq was authorized by the Security Council were heroic. He could do so without fear of censure or sanction by the Security Council because the UK has a veto. A state without a veto wouldn't dare to justify aggression in this way.

To sum up. It is a fundamental principle of international law that states are prohibited from using force except in self-defence or unless its use is formally authorized by the Security Council under Chapter VII of the UN Charter.

No country was attacked by Iraq in March 2003 and there were therefore no grounds to go to war with Iraq on grounds of self-defence. The Security Council *never* authorized military action to disarm Iraq of its 'weapons of mass destruction'. Therefore, the attack on Iraq by the United States and the United Kingdom in March 2003 was a war of aggression.

Tony Blair misled Parliament and the British people in order the make the case for aggression against Iraq. We now turn to the consequences of his conduct.

SEVEN

FROM BASRA TO HELMAND PROVINCE

'There was a real danger that we would find that we couldn't support our people, that we would find a platoon cut off and potentially massacred.'

LORD DANNATT, FORMER CHIEF OF THE GENERAL STAFF

Let us now return to the main narrative and the invasion of Iraq in the spring of 2003. The United States did not repeat the methodical tactics of the first Gulf War. Donald Rumsfeld insisted on a highly mobile, opportunistic campaign, bypassing large-scale Iraqi formations and potential bottlenecks (including major cities en route to Baghdad) in order to decapitate Iraq's command and control systems.

These tactics produced a remarkably swift result, but at the cost of leaving large areas unsecured and substantial numbers of

Iraqi soldiers (and their weapons) at large. However, US forces did rapidly secure Iraq's oil infrastructure, with minimal damage, to forestall a repeat of Saddam's deliberate incineration of Kuwaiti oil wells in 1991.

The United States committed 192,000 troops to the invasion, supported by a coalition of forty-six other nations, led by the UK, with over 45,000 troops, but also including two with no armed forces at all, Costa Rica and the tiny Pacific island nation of Palau, a former US dependency.[100] A vital ally for the US was the Kurdish Peshmerga, which supplied 70,000 fighters. Although Turkey disrupted the US plan by refusing use of its territory, the United States managed to drop several thousand paratroops to help the Kurds to open a second front against Saddam in the north.[101]

The Iraqis were outgunned and led extremely badly by Saddam and his sons, and generals appointed for loyalty rather than competence. They nonetheless managed some stiff resistance at Nasiriyah, Najaf and, especially, the approaches to Basra, which were the main theatres for British forces. Crucially, the US military deceived Saddam's son Uday and captured the strategic city of Karbala, routing Saddam's elite Republican Guard and creating a gap through which they could launch a rapid drive to Baghdad. The capital fell on 9 April 2003 after a protracted battle for the airport. Saddam and his clique disappeared. Baghdadis celebrated by defacing or destroying Saddam's many monuments and gigantic portraits, including the highly publicized toppling

---

100 'Palau, Costa Rica Join US-led Coalition', UPI, 21 March 2003.

101 See Major I. J. Peltier, 'Surrogate Warfare: The Role of US Army Special Forces', US School of Advanced Military Studies, Fort Leavenworth, Kansas, 2005.

of his statue in Firdos Square. On 15 April the US forces took control of Tikrit, the centre of Saddam's clan powerbase.

On 1 May President Bush announced the end of combat operations, posing as a fighter pilot on the US aircraft carrier *Abraham Lincoln* in front of the 'Mission Accomplished' poster which would soon become infamous.

The collapse of Saddam's regime and security apparatus paved the way for widespread looting and sectarian violence, and the settling of old scores, in all of Iraq's major cities. The most highly publicized episode was the looting of the National Museum in Baghdad, but other targets included offices, factories and hospitals, and essential power and water installations. Within Baghdad US forces protected only the Oil Ministry and the Ministry of the Interior (both of vital importance to the occupation). The US has estimated the damage from looting in the first weeks after the invasion at $12 billion.[102] In a press conference on 11 April Rumsfeld did nothing to improve the picture coming from Iraq, dismissing the destruction and looting in a throwaway phrase, 'stuff happens'.[103]

The Bush administration, however, had made scant plans for the administration of Iraq. Scarcely weeks before the war, the Defense Department had created an Office for Humanitarian and Reconstruction Assistance (OHRA), under General Jay Garner. He spoke Arabic and had some understanding of Iraq, especially the Kurdish areas. But Garner's team had few resources and its role had been limited to coping with displaced persons and repairing

---

102 See M. Lamani and B. Momani (eds), *From Desolation to Reconstruction: Iraq's Troubled Journey.* Wilfrid Laurier Univserity Press, 2010, Chapter 7.

103 'Rumsfeld on Looting in Iraq – "Stuff Happens"', CNN.com, 12 April 2003.

oil wells. The OHRA was quickly upgraded into the Coalition Provisional Administration (CPA), a short-term central government. However, Garner lost friends among the administration when he planned for elections in Iraq within ninety days and an early hand-over of power to an Iraqi government.[104] In May, he was replaced by Paul Bremer, a career diplomat close to the neoconservatives around Bush. He did not speak Arabic and had no experience of Iraq. Bremer ruled by decree, and had as much power as General MacArthur wielded in Japan in the aftermath of the Second World War. He answered only to Rumsfeld and President Bush.

Bremer made two early decisions which have provoked intense controversy ever since: the decommissioning of the Iraqi army and the de-Baathification programme to remove members of the ruling party from Iraq's surviving public administration. The first was widely blamed for contributing support and weapons for the later insurgency (although Bremer and others argued that the Iraqi army had effectively dissolved itself before he even arrived). The second was blamed for depriving Iraq's administration and public services of essential talent, since membership of the Baath Party had been a requirement for holding many essential posts in the civilian bureaucracy.

BRITAIN IN SOUTHERN IRAQ

The British had originally been detailed to join the northern offensive. At the very last minute we were diverted to the south

---

104   See 'Sorting the Bad from the Not so Bad', *Time*, 19 May 2003.

– a totally different theatre in terms of topography, climate, ethnicity and politics. It created a whole set of new problems, for which the British had no time to prepare. Surprisingly, the switch was actually welcomed by the UK's military planners. The then Chief of the Defence Staff Lord Boyce later told the Chilcot Inquiry:

> The UK's area of responsibility was seen as a move in the direction of de-risking, as we would have greater control of our own destiny both in the conflict and aftermath phases. It would allow the US forces to make best speed towards Baghdad knowing their rear was covered.[105]

Britain had accepted responsibility for control of four provinces in the southern zone of Iraq. This meant that British forces would have to provide security for an area around 20 per cent greater than the whole of Ireland.

It included Basra, within a total provincial population of around three million people. Blair told the Chilcot Inquiry: 'It meant that we would be in a position of authority in the South. This was desirable since our forces and personnel would be there. We wanted to be in a position of maximum influence. There was no suggestion that this was beyond our capabilities provided of course we got others to come in alongside us; which they did.'[106]

---

105 Lord Boyce, written statement to the Iraq Inquiry, 27 January 2011, pp. 1–2
     http://www.iraqinquiry.org.uk/media/51158/Boyce-Statement.pdf.
106 Tony Blair, written statement to the Iraq Inquiry, 14 January 2011, p. 18
     http://www.iraqinquiry.org.uk/media/50743/Blair-statement.pdf.

To start with it appeared as though Blair's optimism, backed by the military leadership, would be justified. British forces were reduced from their peak of over 45,000 at the invasion to 12,000 in the autumn and about 8,000 by the end of the year. They were supported by multinational forces, led by the Italians and the Dutch, whose maximum strength was 5,500.[107] By contrast the allies had committed 60,000 soldiers to Kosovo in 1999,[108] an area less than one-ninth the size of southern Iraq, with much easier communications and a far more friendly population.

Much of the analysis which follows is drawn from two strongly argued books by Frank Ledwidge, a former military intelligence officer who served in both Iraq and Afghanistan: *Losing Small Wars* (2011) and *Investment in Blood* (2013), both published by Yale University Press. Ledwidge exposes the political and military hubris which pushed British forces into unachievable missions with calamitous consequences.

In the early months of the occupation British soldiers patrolled Basra in soft hats and enjoyed its cosmopolitan café society.[109] The British force in the south did not have the fighting strength to do much more – by far their greatest number were administrative, technical and other support staff. The British had little intelligence about local factions: some of the staff who might have provided this were diverted to the fruitless search for Saddam's weapons of mass destruction. Reconstruction activity was slow

---

107 See the reply by Defence Minister Lord Bach to Lord Williams of Elvel, on 16 July 2003, HL 127-29W.

108 This telling comparison is made by Frank Ledwidge, *Losing Small Wars*, Yale University Press, 2011, p. 65.

109 Ibid., p. 23.

and sporadic and tasks identified as immediate priorities, such as organizing refuse collection and inspecting electricity sub-stations, were not undertaken. Above all, the British could not provide any basic security for local people.[110]

Throughout 2003 Blair and his generals contrasted the apparent calm in Basra with the growing Sunni insurgency in the US-run zone. In the early months there were merely isolated attacks on US troops in Baghdad, Fallujah and Tikrit. In June 2003 Donald Rumsfeld attributed the situation to 'pockets of dead-enders' (i.e. residual Saddam loyalists).

The insurgency entered a new phase in August with attacks on the Jordanian embassy, the UN Mission and the Shia Imam Ali Mosque in the holy city of Najaf. The last of these killed the high-ranking Shia cleric Ayatollah Mohammed Baqir al-Hakim. These attacks signalled a more ambitious insurgent agenda of making Iraq ungovernable under the occupation and instigating a civil war against the Shia. Insurgent operations became more deadly with more advanced forms of improvised explosive device (IED), mortar and rocket attacks, and better-prepared ambushes. This period of the occupation also saw a rise in attacks by suicide bombers. The capture of Saddam Hussein in December did nothing to abate the violence.

Britain's army chief of staff General Sir Mike Jackson thought the Americans' military posture ('in their Darth Vader kit' as Sir John Sawers termed it) contributed to their problems in Baghdad. He proposed bringing a paratroop battalion to the city to show

110 Ibid., pp. 23–8.

them how to do peacekeeping. But this, arguably, patronizing plan never came to fruition.[111] Tony Blair visited Basra in January 2004, where he was photographed with British soldiers (his pro-consul, Sir Hilary Synnott, had a stand-up row with Blair's media team to prevent him from snubbing the local Iraqi governor).[112] Blair pronounced himself delighted with the British-built police academy, clearly unaware that the newly trained police were violent and corrupt.[113]

British optimism vanished on 6 April 2004. In three of the four British-run provinces Shia militias erupted into full-scale insurgency. They were reacting to two US decisions over which the British had no influence: the assault on Fallujah and a confrontation with the militant Shia figure Muqtada al-Sadr, the leader of the Mahdi army.

The British commander, Major General Andrew Stewart, later said 'it was like a switch had been flicked'. He described to the Chilcot Inquiry how he had had to react to the news of thirty-five militia attacks before 7.30 in the morning and to their capture of the town of Nasiriya in the neighbouring province of Al-Amara, which was assigned to the Italian military contingent.

Stewart's forces were strung out over two provinces. He decided that he must regain control of Nasiriya to support the

---

111   Ibid., p. 31. And see Sir John Sawers in evidence to the Chilcot Inquiry, http://www.iraqinquiry.org.uk/media/40668/20091210amsawers-final.pdf pp. 82–4.

112   H. Synnott, *Bad Days in Basra*, IB Tauris, 2008, p. 147.

113   T. Blair, *A Journey*, Arrow, 2011, p. 468. The British commander, Major General Andrew Stewart, later told the Chilcot Inquiry that the police were 'absolutely untrainable. We should have got rid of them and kept the army, not the other way round' (Transcript of evidence, 9 December 2009, p. 75).

Italians, but in Basra 'tried to get an Iraqi solution through the council… we absolutely had to keep the consent of the Basra people, because if we lost that we did not have the force even to remain in Basra, we would have been unable to operate.'[114]

It was the only possible decision. But it confirmed that the British were not in control of the city: effectively it was abandoned to Shia militias. Inspired by a false analogy with Northern Ireland, the British actually recruited many of these into the police, which gave them a licence for extortion and ethnic cleansing of the city's Sunni and Christian minorities. The worst of them operated under the ironic title of the Serious Crimes Unit.[115] Meanwhile, outside the city, British soldiers were attacked with growing frequency and sophistication, as Shia insurgents made use of more sophisticated IEDs supplied by Iran.

In September 2006, the British launched a major attempt to reconquer Basra from the Shiite militias. Called Operation Sinbad, the operation briefly suppressed some of the worst excesses by the local police but it ended in February 2007 after forty-six British deaths with the Shia militias completely in control of the city.[116]

Thereafter the British endured repeated attacks on their lone garrison in the centre of the city. By July 2007 (after Gordon Brown had finally ousted Tony Blair as prime minister) we were losing a serviceman every four days. Eventually, we swallowed a bitter pill and negotiated a complete withdrawal from the city with the imprisoned leader of the leading Shiite militia.

---

114 Transcript of evidence, 9 December 2009, pp. 68–70.
115 Ledwidge, *Losing Small Wars*, pp. 33–4.
116 See J. Newsinger, *British Counterinsurgency*, Palgrave, 2015, pp. 228–9.

For the remainder of the year British troops hunkered down at their giant base at the airport, with no influence on events in southern Iraq, attracting scarcely concealed contempt from the Americans and the new Iraqi leader, Nouri al-Maliki.[117] This posture contrasted starkly with the US 'surge' ordered by Bush and conducted with considerable military and political skill by General David Petraeus. With help from British SAS units, and even more from Sunni former insurgents who decided to turn on al-Qaeda, General Petraeus managed to check civil war and terrorism and provide a breathing space for painstaking negotiations on a new Iraqi constitution.

The British withdrawal from Basra was described as a deliberate change of role to 'overwatch' duties, but it delivered the city and all its essential economic resources into the hands of rival militias and gangsters. Al-Maliki decided on his own initiative to recapture the city. He bypassed the British and even surprised Petraeus by launching a major offensive in March 2008 with newly trained and equipped security forces, under the grandiose title of Operation Charge of the Knights.

Al-Maliki's inexperienced 14th Division was badly mauled by the Iranian-armed militia but was hastily backed by the Americans, who supported a counter-attack by the 1st Division. The British remained at a distance from the fighting, at Basra airport, but gave some help with reconnaissance and medical aid. The counter-attack was successful and after a brief pause, brokered by the militia's Iranian patrons, the Iraqis resumed

---

117 Ibid., p. 229, Ledwidge, *Losing Small Wars*, pp. 53–5.

operations in April and eventually regained control of the entire city. Al-Maliki developed an abiding mistrust of the British, while a number of ordinary Basrawis continued to blame them for all of their misfortunes.[118]

British troops lingered on in southern Iraq in a training and support role until July 2009 when their final withdrawal paved the way for the start of the Chilcot Inquiry. By then the British had lost 179 men in Iraq and thousands more had suffered lasting physical or psychological damage.

THE SWITCH TO HELMAND

This was the unpromising background to the British decision to boost its forces in Afghanistan. The move was announced on 26 January 2006, when Defence Secretary John Reid declared that a provincial reconstruction team (PRT) would go to Helmand province in the south of Afghanistan, supported by a force of 3,300 troops backed by artillery and advanced Apache attack helicopters.

The prime British tasks there would be to secure control of the province for Afghan President Karzai, and to suppress opium production. With the exception of the veteran Conservative Sir Peter Tapsell no MPs raised any fundamental doubts about this new commitment or the scale of the force sent to fulfil it.[119]

In his evidence to the Chilcot Inquiry Sir Richard Dannatt,

---

118 Ledwidge, *Losing Small Wars*, pp. 53–5 and M. Cochrane, 'Operation Knight's Charge', published by the Institute for the Study of War, Washington DC, 2009.

119 See *Hansard*, House of Commons Debates, 26 January 2006, Cols 1528–48.

former chief of the General Staff, claimed that the move came as a surprise to him: '"Wow, where did that come from?", I think was my feeling at the time.'[120] However, Tony Blair in his memoirs wrote 'the military chiefs, *dismayed at the limits of what we could do in Iraq*, [author's emphasis], were increasingly wanting to switch emphasis from Iraq to Afghanistan'.[121]

There was no good reason for Helmand to be assigned to the UK. In fact, there were strong historic and psychological reasons for the British to stay out of it. Helmand was the site of a famous Afghan victory over the British in 1880 at Maiwand, which was an enduring symbol of local resistance to foreigners.[122]

However, Helmand was also a fertile area for the cultivation of the opium poppy and Tony Blair had volunteered Britain to take the lead in international anti-narcotic initiatives in Afghanistan. Blair had in effect committed the British to win over a difficult province to a remote central government while eliminating its main source of revenue.[123]

The British insisted on the dismissal of the local governor, Sher Mohammed Akhundzada. He had ruled brutally as an old-fashioned warlord, and the British believed that he was heavily implicated in the narcotics trade. But he had kept a lid on the province. Sher Mohammed responded to his dismissal by releasing 3,000 of his private army (almost equal to the British force

---

120 http://www.iraqinquiry.org.uk/media/55298/20100728am-dannatt.pdf p. 14.
121 Blair, *A Journey*, p. 610.
122 F. Ledwidge, *Investment in Blood*, Yale University Press, 2013, pp. 25–6.
123 Around the end of 2001 Tony Blair decreed to Whitehall that opium poppy cultivation in Afghanistan should be eliminated within ten years. This decree was characteristic. It betrayed the ignorance of Afghan society and the Afghan economy, while indicating a naïve faith in Soviet-style numerical targets.

in Helmand) to the local Taliban in order to save their wages.[124] He was replaced as governor by Mohammed Daoud, commonly known as Engineer Daoud, who was an honest, diligent man but lacking a private army. He would need the British to conquer his province for him.

The British were hoping to achieve their mission with just 3,300 troops. Moreover, as had been the case in Basra only a few hundred of these were available for combat at any one time.[125] The remainder were necessary technical, logistic and other support staff, who had to be accommodated in a large fortified camp. Essentially, as in Basra, the British army was reduced to making sorties from its base to establish temporary garrisons under constant harassing enemy fire. Particularly in Helmand it had to substitute firepower for manpower simply to defend itself, unable to discriminate between real enemies and the civilian population – and turning the latter into the former.

Engineer Daoud was amazed and disappointed by the combat strength of the British force. However, he continued to demand that it spread out to provide security and wrest control of towns from hostile warlords and militias. The United States was making similar demands. Under pressure from both, the British abandoned their initial (and justified) caution in Helmand and moved into the town of Sangin, where they would take terrible punishment from the Taliban. 'Our resources were stretched to breaking point', British commander Colonel Stuart Tootal recalled. For General Dannatt, 'There was a real danger that we would find

124 Ledwidge, *Losing Small Wars*, pp. 65–6.
125 Ibid., p. 72.

that we couldn't support our people, that we would find a platoon cut off and potentially massacred.'[126]

In southern Iraq, the British army could not fulfil the basic duties of an occupying power, to protect life and property, let alone help to transform the conquered territory into part of a modern democratic state. In Helmand, it could not wrest the territory and population of the province, or even a small part of them, from the hands of hostile warlords or the Taliban.

As British casualties mounted with no visible gains from their sacrifice, government ministers were hard put to explain their mission. Eventually they hit on an explanation which was in its way as misleading as anything put out by Tony Blair in the run-up to the invasion of Iraq.

The defence secretary, John Hutton, claimed that British troops were in Afghanistan to prevent al-Qaeda using the country as a base to attack British streets.[127] This line was echoed by all the party leaders when they joined in paying personal tributes at Prime Minister's Question Time to dead soldiers they had never known.[128] It was nonsense. Al-Qaeda was virtually non-existent in Helmand and the local Taliban had neither the will nor the capability to launch terrorist operations on British soil.[129]

---

126 Interviewed for *Afghanistan: The Lion's Last Roar?* BBC2, broadcast 26 October 2014.

127 'I am absolutely clear that our commitment to Afghanistan is first and foremost about the UK's national security.' John Hutton, speech at the International Institute for Strategic Studies, 11 November 2008, http://news.bbc.co.uk/1/hi/uk/7725228.stm.

128 This practice was introduced by Tony Blair in 2005. It was continued by Gordon Brown, who also introduced Armed Forces Day and other distinctly unBritish gestures of glorification of the services.

129 Ledwidge, *Investment in Blood*, pp. 203–4.

In 2009 the British lost 108 soldiers in Helmand, while many more sustained permanent injury. Their casualty rate was four times higher than that suffered by the US military. In early 2010 they were relieved by a larger and better-equipped force of US Marines, as part of an Afghan 'surge' ordered by President Obama.

By this stage, British forces had sustained 453 dead, over 2,600 physically wounded and at least 5,000 with lasting psychological damage. They had managed to 'stabilize' three of fourteen districts of a province which had been stable (although badly governed) before they arrived, comprising about 1 per cent of the territory of Afghanistan. Opium production had risen during the time of Britain's tenure in Helmand, from 40 per cent of Afghanistan's total output to nearly a half.[130]

LESSONS FROM IRAQ AND AFGHANISTAN

In both Basra and Helmand, British soldiers were victims of the hubris of their military and political leaders. They were sent as supposed 'liberators' to countries with a historic legacy of hatred for Britain as an invader and occupier. Their leaders were almost wholly ignorant of the people they were meant to be liberating and the conditions under which they lived. Our forces were given grandiose and contradictory objectives with nothing like the resources required to achieve them. They were hampered in each case by a confused command structure and a system of

---

130 Newsinger, *British Counterinsurgency*, pp. 240–1; Ledwidge, *Investment in Blood*, pp. 215–20.

short-term deployments which ensured inconsistent policy and repeated failure to learn from repeated mistakes.

In each adventure, British forces were reduced to desperate defensive measures, in which they abandoned the local populations they were sent to protect, and from which they had to be relieved by the Americans, whom their leaders had hoped to impress. Each intervention left their enemies stronger than before.

Each adventure inflicted huge costs on the British taxpayer with no compensating benefit of any kind. Each cost the lives of hundreds of soldiers and left thousands more permanently wounded physically and mentally. Although their government initiated a cult around the armed forces, abetted by some of the tabloid press, many survivors felt a lasting estrangement from the people at home who had no understanding of their experience.

Each intervention produced uncounted casualties among local people, and left them a prey to violence and extortion from local gangs and warlords and sectarian factions, often in the guise of police officers or security services operating under licence from the British.

Instead of learning anything from the growing disaster in Basra, Britain's leaders were only too eager to repeat it in Helmand. That is because each had a common motive, from both a military and a political point of view: to retain Britain's status and supposed influence as the most valued ally of the United States. Even this objective was not achieved. The Americans took away from each adventure an enduring impression of British arrogance and inadequacy.

Broadly speaking, this is the argument of Frank Ledwidge's two books. Ledwidge focused strongly on failures of military leadership. He emphasized the profusion of senior officers with too little to do except defend the interests of their service (and their own careers) and the prevalence of obsolete military doctrines of counter-insurgency based on irrelevant and inaccurate comparisons with past experience in Malaya and Northern Ireland. Although often brutal in his assessment of their military skills, Ledwidge often admires the generals' astuteness in politics and public relations, particularly their ability to pin setbacks, and British casualties, on politicians' failure to provide enough kit.

Ledwidge is a little too kind to the politicians. It was their responsibility to give our forces missions with worthwhile motives and achievable tasks and to see through any false optimism about the force levels required. No member of Tony Blair's government measured up to that responsibility.

EIGHT

HOW MI5 WAS RIGHT ABOUT AL-QAEDA AND IRAQ

'[T]he JIC [Joint Intelligence Committee] judged that the build-up of forces in the Gulf, in the region, prior to an attack on Iraq, would increase public hostility to the West and Western interests.'

SIR DAVID OMAND IN EVIDENCE
TO THE CHILCOT INQUIRY

Britain went to war with the declared aim of removing the threat of Saddam Hussein's weapons of mass destruction in order to make the world, including Britain, a safer place. At least, that's what Tony Blair told us.

In his final speech to Parliament on the eve of war, the prime minister highlighted the risk that terrorist groups could link up with murderous regimes such as Saddam Hussein's Iraq:

'The possibility of the two coming together – of terrorist groups in possession of weapons of mass destruction or even of a so-called dirty radiological bomb – is now, in my judgement, a real and present danger to Britain and its national security.'[131]

So it is important to ask whether the invasion of Iraq made British streets safer. The evidence given to Chilcot was terrifyingly clear on this point. Baroness Eliza Manningham-Buller was the director general of MI5, the UK's domestic intelligence agency, from October 2002 until April 2007 – that is, for a few months before the US/UK invasion of Iraq and for four years afterwards, while the US and the UK were occupying Iraq. She gave evidence to the Chilcot Inquiry on 20 July 2010.[132]

In answer to the question 'to what extent did the conflict in Iraq exacerbate the overall threat that your Service and your fellow services were having to deal with from international terrorism?' she replied, 'Substantially'.[133] Baroness Manningham-Buller said there was hard evidence for this, for instance 'numerical evidence of the number of plots, the number of leads, the number of people identified, and the correlation of that to Iraq and statements of people as to why they were involved, the discussions between them as to what they were doing'.[134]

Baroness Manningham-Buller produced one extraordinary fact which substantiated her assertion that the threat had increased following March 2003. She had been forced to ask Tony Blair for a *doubling* of the MI5 budget in the aftermath of the Iraq

131 *Hansard*, House of Commons Debates, 18 March 2003, Col 768.
132 www.iraqinquiry.org.uk/media/48331/20100720am-manningham-buller.pdf.
133 Ibid., pp. 24–5.
134 Ibid., p. 34.

invasion. She told the inquiry: 'This is unheard of, it's certainly unheard of today, but he and the Treasury and the Chancellor accepted that because I was able to demonstrate the scale of the problem that we were confronted by.'[135]

Sir Roderic Lyne asked her how significant 'a factor was Iraq compared with other situations that were used by extremists, terrorists, to justify their actions', to which she replied, 'I think it is highly significant'.[136] There had been, she said, 'an increasing number of British-born individuals living and brought up in this country, some of them third generation, who were attracted to the ideology of Osama bin Laden and saw the West's activities in Iraq and Afghanistan as threatening their fellow religionists and the Muslim world'.[137]

As a consequence, the fact that the London bombings in July 2005 were carried out by British citizens didn't come as a surprise to MI5. There is no doubt whatsoever that al-Qaeda-related activity in Britain increased 'substantially' because of Britain's participation in the invasion of Iraq. This activity included the bombings of 7 July 2005, in which fifty-two people were killed and more than 700 were injured.

If Britain had not participated in the invasion of Iraq, it is very unlikely that such an upsurge in al-Qaeda-related activity in Britain, including the bombings, would have occurred. Stating that is not a justification for the bombings or other al-Qaeda attacks. It is simply a statement of probability.

---

135 Ibid., pp. 26–7.
136 Ibid., p. 18.
137 Ibid., p. 19.

SIR DAVID OMAND'S
EVIDENCE TO CHILCOT

The Chilcot Inquiry also heard that in advance of the invasion
of Iraq, the UK intelligence services warned that the threat to
Britain from terrorism was likely to be heightened as a result
of British participation in the invasion of Iraq.

Sir David Omand held the post of security and intelligence co-
ordinator in the Cabinet Office from June 2002 until April 2005.
He gave evidence to the inquiry on 20 January 2010. Chilcot
panellist Sir Lawrence Freedman asked what intelligence assessments were made before the invasion about the potential impact
on al-Qaeda. Sir David replied:

> In August 2002, the JIC [Joint Intelligence Committee] judged
> that the build-up of forces in the Gulf, in the region, prior to
> an attack on Iraq, would increase public hostility to the West
> and Western interests.
>
> By 10 October the JIC is warning that AQ [al-Qaeda] and
> other Islamist extremists may initiate attacks in response to
> coalition military action. We [the intelligence services] pointed
> out that AQ would use an attack on Iraq as justification ... for
> terrorist attacks on Western or Israeli targets. We pointed out
> that AQ was already in their propaganda portraying US-led oper-
> ations as being a war on Islam and that, indeed, this view was
> attracting widespread support across the Muslim community.
>
> Coalition attacks would, we said, radicalize increasing
> numbers. On 16 October 2002, we reaffirmed that the United

Kingdom was a priority target for AQ. On 13 December 2002, we warned that US-led action could draw large numbers to the Islamist extremist ideology over the following five years, and again, on 10 February, that the threat from AQ would increase at the onset of any attack on Iraq and that we should all be prepared for a higher threat level to be announced and for more terrorist activity in the event of war.[138]

In her evidence Baroness Manningham-Buller endorsed Sir David Omand's evidence. She revealed that she had also warned in advance that there was likely to be a heightened threat from al-Qaeda as a result of British participation in the invasion of Iraq. She agreed that her judgement prior to the invasion was that 'a war in Iraq would aggravate the [terrorist] threat from whatever source to the United Kingdom' and that 'there wasn't any particular controversy amongst the intelligence agencies about that judgement'.[139]

This warning was communicated to the government through Joint Intelligence Committee (JIC) assessments and, in her case, directly to the home secretary (David Blunkett at the time) to whom the head of MI5 reports. If ministers read JIC assessments, she said, 'they can have had no doubt' that, in the opinion of the intelligence services, the projected invasion of Iraq would increase the threat to Britain from al-Qaeda.[140]

---

138 www.iraqinquiry.org.uk/media/44187/20100120pm-omand-final.pdf, pp.38–9.
139 www.iraqinquiry.org.uk/media/48331/20100720am-manningham-buller.
      pdf, pp. 31–32.
140 Ibid., p. 33.

GOVERNMENT STAYED SILENT ABOUT HEIGHTENED THREAT PREDICTION

The government was very keen to bring intelligence assessments of the alleged threat from Iraq's weapons of mass destruction to public attention. By contrast it kept silent about the pre-war intelligence assessments that the al-Qaeda threat to Britain would be heightened by British participation in military action against Iraq. The reason for this is pretty obvious: the government was in the business of making a case for war against Iraq, so intelligence assessments that suggested that this would increase the likelihood of bombs in British streets were kept from Parliament and the public. Had MPs been aware of these assessments on 18 March 2003, they might not have given a green light to military action.

On that day, Tony Blair did not tell them that al-Qaeda activity in Britain would likely increase with murderous effect if they voted for war. On the contrary, he told them that a vote for war was a vote to combat terrorism; that the overthrow of Saddam Hussein would impede a future alliance between him and terrorists, as a consequence of which terrorists would be armed with 'weapons of mass destruction'.

This was a variant of the story told by the Bush administration at the time to bolster popular support for attacking Iraq, namely, that such an alliance already existed and Saddam Hussein had a hand in the 9/11 attacks. This was and is not supported by any intelligence. Nevertheless, a Harris poll in July 2006 suggested that two out of three Americans still believed it to be true. And, according to a Zogby poll in February 2006, 85 per cent of the

US troops serving in Iraq believed that their mission was mainly 'to retaliate for Saddam's role in the 9/11 attacks'.[141]

BRITISH VERSION OF THE US PROPAGANDA LINE

Alastair Campbell was Tony Blair's communications chief. His diary entry for 27 February 2003 explains why the British version of the US propaganda line was adopted:

> TB felt we had to be pushing on two main arguments – the moral case and the reason why the threat was real and current, not because he could whack missiles off at London but because he could tie up with terrorists and others with a vested interest in damaging us and our interests. But we should understate rather than overstate … The Americans' saying there was a direct link [between terrorists and Saddam Hussein] was counterproductive. Far better to be saying there was a possibility and one that we were determined to ensure never came about.[142]

How a non-existent alliance could pose a threat that is 'real and current' remains a mystery.

Nevertheless this propaganda line (including the assertion that Britain was under threat from a non-existent alliance) appeared

---

141 See David Morrison, 'Al-Qaeda, ISIS, and the wider fallout from the Iraq invasion', openDemocracy, 28 October 2015, https://www.opendemocracy.net/uk/david-morrison/al-qaeda-isis-and-wider-fallout-from-iraq-invasion.

142 A. Campbell, *The Alastair Campbell Diaries, Vol. 4*, Hutchinson, 2012, p. 469.

in Tony Blair's speech on 18 March 2003 when he persuaded the House of Commons to endorse military action:

> The key today is stability and order. The threat is chaos and disorder – and there are two begetters of chaos: tyrannical regimes with weapons of mass destruction and extreme terrorist groups who profess a perverted and false view of Islam …
>
> Those two threats have, of course, different motives and different origins, but they share one basic common view: they detest the freedom, democracy and tolerance that are the hallmarks of our way of life. At the moment, I accept fully that the association between the two is loose – but it is hardening. The possibility of the two coming together – of terrorist groups in possession of weapons of mass destruction or even of a so-called dirty radiological bomb – is now, in my judgement, a real and present danger to Britain and its national security.

Tony Blair didn't mention to the House of Commons on that day that he had recently received an intelligence assessment titled *International Terrorism: War with Iraq*,[143] which:

1. said that there was no intelligence that Iraq had provided chemical or biological (CB) materials to al-Qaeda or of Iraqi intentions to conduct CB terrorist attacks using Iraqi intelligence officials or their agents;
2. judged that in the event of imminent regime collapse there

---

143 ISC report, www.official-documents.gov.uk/document/cm59/5972/5972.pdf, paragraph 126.

would be a risk of transfer of such material, whether or not as a deliberate Iraqi regime policy;

3. assessed that al-Qaeda and associated groups continued to represent by far the greatest terrorist threat to Western interests, and that threat would be heightened by military action against Iraq.

Tony Blair didn't tell the House of Commons any of this on 18 March 2003 before MPs voted for military action against Iraq.

VERDICT

Saddam Hussein was ideologically opposed to al-Qaeda and didn't allow it to operate in the part of Iraq under his control (though an al-Qaeda-related group, Ansar al-Islam, operated in Kurdish-controlled northern Iraq). The notion of an alliance between Saddam and al-Qaeda was a fantasy invented to provide some sort of an answer to the question: why are you invading Iraq, when you say that the greatest threat to the West is al-Qaeda?

The pragmatic thing for the US to do after 9/11 was to make peace with Saddam Hussein's Iraq, a secular Arab state opposed to al-Qaeda, and with Iran, a Shia state opposed to al-Qaeda – and do what was necessary to force Saudi Arabia and its Gulf state allies to cease providing inspiration to al-Qaeda.

But, instead, Iran was included in the 'axis of evil' and shunned by the US and its allies, and Iraq was invaded and occupied, falsely justified in part on the grounds that Saddam Hussein was one of the architects of 9/11 – and in the process Iraq was transformed from an al-Qaeda-free zone into an area where Islamist extremism flourished, so much so that the US president later described it as 'the central front in the war on terror'.[144] Meanwhile, Saudi Arabia has continued to inspire al-Qaeda and its offshoots – and continues to be the US's best friend in the Middle East.

This disastrous policy, which has cost the lives of hundreds of thousands of Iraqis, was compounded in the following decade by the overthrow of another secular Arab regime in Libya in 2011, followed by a long attempt to overthrow another in Syria. Three secular Arab states that were potential allies against al-Qaeda have been destroyed or badly damaged by the US and its allies, enthusiastically supported by Britain. And as a direct consequence of this instability and power vacuum, the al-Qaeda offshoot, ISIS (the so-called Islamic State or Daesh), has established a 'caliphate' in parts of Iraq and Syria, and has associated organizations in many parts of the Muslim world, from Nigeria to Libya, to Yemen and Afghanistan.

---

144 http://georgewbush-whitehouse.archives.gov/news/releases/2005/11/
20051130-2.html.

NINE

THE CHILCOT INQUIRY
AND ITS ANTECEDENTS

*'I am satisfied that Mr Scarlett, the other members
of the JIC, and the members of the assessment staff
engaged in the drafting of the dossier were concerned to
ensure that the contents of the dossier were consistent
with the intelligence available to the JIC.'*

LORD HUTTON

In Chapter 7 we charted the fortunes of British troops in southern Iraq in the years from 2003 up to the desperate withdrawal from Basra in 2007, and then the bloody engagement in Afghanistan.

We have not yet told the story of political events at Westminster after the invasion of Iraq. In the immediate aftermath, the Downing Street press machine choreographed a set of exclusive interviews and photo-opportunities with the prime minister. These exploited the apparent success of the war for political purposes.

The BBC's then political editor Andrew Marr recorded that Tony Blair 'stands as a larger man and a stronger prime minister as a result'. Marr told BBC viewers that the war drew the line under 'a faint air of pointlessness' which had been hanging over Downing Street: 'There were all these slightly tawdry arguments and scandals. That is now history.'[145]

The triumphalist mood did not last. The post-war ebullience inside Downing Street quickly dissipated. The first problem concerned the *casus belli*, weapons of mass destruction. No one in Iraq could find any trace of them, not even the most gullible journalists or compliant intelligence agents.[146] The failure to discover weapons of mass destruction raised extremely embarrassing questions about the quality of the intelligence used to justify the invasion, and led to a series of inquiries. First to report was the Foreign Affairs Committee of the House of Commons.

On 3 June 2003, the Foreign Affairs Committee (FAC) announced an inquiry into the government's decision to go to

---

145 P. Oborne, *The Triumph of the Political Class*, Simon & Schuster, 2007, pp. 291–2.

146 On 28 January 2004, David Kay, the former head of the Iraq Survey Group, the organization established by the US to search for WMD in Iraq, reported to the US Congress: 'Prior to the war, my view was that the best evidence that I had seen was that Iraq, indeed, had weapons of mass destruction. I would also point out that many governments that chose not to support this war – certainly the French President Chirac, referred to Iraq's possession of WMD. The German intelligence certainly believed that there was WMD. It turns out that we were all wrong, probably in my judgement, and that is most disturbing' (see edition.cnn.com/2004/US/01/28/kay.transcript/). The Iraq Survey Group was disbanded in 2005 having spent at least $1 billion in failing to find WMD in Iraq.

war in Iraq. Its stated terms of reference were to consider whether the government 'presented accurate and complete information to Parliament in the period leading up to military action in Iraq, particularly in relation to Iraq's weapons of mass destruction'.[147]

A month later, on 7 July 2003, the FAC found the government not guilty: 'we conclude that Ministers did not mislead Parliament'.[148]

To call this inquiry a whitewash is to praise it too highly. The committee spent most of its time (and nearly half its report) trying to answer a question it was incapable of answering, namely, whether the claims in the government's dossier on Iraq's weapons of mass destruction published in September 2002 were justified by the intelligence available at the time.

It wasn't in a position to answer that question because the government denied it access to the intelligence and to the people responsible for assessing the intelligence and drawing up the dossier. The committee was groping in the dark. To be fair, the committee complained about this in paragraph 90 of its report, which said: 'We conclude that without access to the intelligence or to those who handled it, we cannot know if it was in any respect faulty or misinterpreted.'

So, by its own admission, the committee could not know if the intelligence on which the September dossier was based was 'in any respect faulty or misinterpreted'. Nevertheless, it concluded

---

147 nsarchive.gwu.edu/NSAEBB/NSAEBB80/wmd34.pdf.
148 Ibid., paragraph 186. That verdict was hardly unexpected, since the committee was chaired by a Blair loyalist, Donald Anderson MP, and seven out of its eleven members were Labour MPs, though two of them and the one Liberal Democrat member had voted against military action.

that the intelligence was not misinterpreted. It didn't say how it achieved this impossible feat.[149]

The Intelligence and Security Committee (ISC) did a slightly better job. In May 2003 it set out to 'examine whether the available intelligence, which informed the decision to invade Iraq, was adequate and properly assessed and whether it was accurately reflected in Government publications'.[150] It reported in September 2003.

Unlike the FAC, the ISC had access to the relevant intelligence and was therefore in a position to judge if the September dossier was an accurate summary of that intelligence. Many of its conclusions were helpful to the government. However, its report of 11 September 2003 was very revealing about the gaps and uncertainties in the intelligence about Iraq's proscribed weapons, and the degree to which these gaps and uncertainties were glossed over in the September dossier to paint a more coherent and threatening picture than was justified by the intelligence.

John Scarlett, the chairman of the Joint Intelligence Committee (JIC), insisted to the ISC (and later to the Hutton Inquiry) that

---

149 As we have seen, the House of Commons failed to expose misrepresentations by Tony Blair in the House of Commons on 18 March 2003, even though at the time there was ample information in the public domain to do so. In November 2003, David Morrison made a submission to the committee on the glaring inadequacy of its report, listing a host of matters it failed to consider (see www.publications.parliament.uk/pa/cm200203/cmselect/cmfaff/813/813we26.htm) and in a letter to the committee chair asked for the inquiry to be reopened (see www.publications.parliament.uk/pa/cm200304/cmselect/cmfaff/81/3120218.htm). The letter concluded: 'What is the point of the Committee if it fails to shine a bright light on what was the most important foreign policy decision in a generation?' The inquiry wasn't reopened.

150 https://www.gov.uk/government/uploads/system/uploads/attachment_data/file/272079/5972.pdf.

the dossier was all his committee's work, and not influenced by Downing Street interference. So the ISC criticism falls on him rather than Tony Blair. We now come to the most controversial and tragic of the early reports related to the Iraq War.

THE HUTTON INQUIRY

The most significant of all these inquiries was the Hutton Inquiry, which came about because of a tragedy that no one could have predicted.

As the Foreign Affairs Committee and Intelligence and Security Committee investigations were getting under way, Tony Blair and his communications chief Alastair Campbell were suddenly embarrassed by two stories which accused the government of 'sexing up' the September 2002 dossier to exaggerate the threat from Saddam Hussein. The BBC Radio Four defence correspondent Andrew Gilligan made this claim on the *Today* programme on 29 May 2003, without naming Campbell. Then he made an almost identical claim in the *Mail on Sunday* – and did name Campbell.

Both these reports had their origin in Gilligan's conversations with Dr David Kelly, an expert on biological weapons who was a consultant to the Ministry of Defence.

Whitehall soon unearthed Kelly as the source, whereupon he was offered up as a witness to the ongoing Foreign Affairs Committee inquiry. Kelly was questioned aggressively. A few days later his dead body was discovered in woodlands near his

Oxfordshire home, an apparent suicide. Blair was given this news when flying to Tokyo after a visit to Washington. In genuine shock, but well aware of the uproar the news would cause, he at once set up a new inquiry. On the advice of his new Lord Chancellor (and old friend) Charles Falconer, he chose Lord Hutton, the former chief justice of Northern Ireland, to chair the investigation.[151]

The Hutton Inquiry was established by the government on 18 July 2003 and reported on 28 January 2004. Its terms of reference were 'urgently to conduct an investigation into the circumstances surrounding the death of Dr Kelly'.[152]

Unlike the ISC, Hutton did not examine all the available intelligence on Iraq's 'weapons of mass destruction', and he was therefore not in a position to make a general judgement about the government's use or misuse of that intelligence. But he had access to a wide range of people who were involved in the drawing up of the September dossier, including the chairman of the JIC John Scarlett.

Hutton was directly concerned only with the intelligence, such as it was, that supported the claim in the dossier that Saddam could deploy weapons of mass destruction within forty-five minutes of an order to use them. He was concerned with this because Kelly was the source for Andrew Gilligan's allegation that the government 'sexed up' the dossier by inserting the claim, when it 'probably … knew that the forty-five-minute figure was wrong'.

By now the Intelligence and Security Committee had already

---

151   T. Blair, *A Journey*, Arrow, 2011, p. 459.
152   The Hutton Report, https://fas.org/irp/world/uk/huttonreport.pdf, p. 1.

found that the forty-five-minute claim was based on an MI6 report dated 30 August 2002, which was incorporated into a formal JIC assessment of 9 September 2002.[153] In other words, there was an intelligence basis of sorts for the claim, which was regarded as reliable at the time. Gilligan's allegation that the government had inserted the claim knowing it to be wrong or unreliable was not supported by the evidence. Unsurprisingly, Hutton came to the same conclusion.[154]

Lord Hutton's inquiry remains an important source for anyone wishing to understand the background to the Iraq War. It was especially revelatory about the extent of collusion between the intelligence services and Downing Street officials. It showed how the Downing Street communications chief Alastair Campbell chaired two meetings at which John Scarlett was present. Even very junior members of the Downing Street media team, such as press officer Danny Pruce, were invited to comment on Scarlett's dossier.

The Hutton Inquiry also exposed the way that John Scarlett

---

153 ISC report, www.official-documents.gov.uk/document/cm59/5972/5972.pdf, paragraph 50.

154 Hutton Report, paragraph 228(2), https://fas.org/irp/world/uk/huttonreport. pdf. The following year, during Lord Butler's inquiry into intelligence about Iraq's weapons capability, it emerged that the forty-five-minute claim had come 'third-hand'. In July 2004 Butler concluded that the limitations of the intelligence had not been 'made sufficiently clear', with important caveats removed. The forty-five-minute claim was 'unsubstantiated' and should not have been included without clarification. Doubt was also cast on the links in the reporting chain. On 12 October 2004 the then Foreign Secretary Jack Straw told the House of Commons that MI6 had withdrawn the claim.

gave essential cover to Tony Blair throughout the Kelly controversy. As the crisis broke, Downing Street made a series of false statements about the way the dossier of September 2002 had been prepared. For example, on 4 June 2003 Tony Blair told MPs that 'the allegation that the forty-five-minute claim provoked disquiet among the Intelligence Community, which disagreed with its inclusion in the dossier – I have discussed it, as I said, with the Chairman of the Joint Intelligence Committee – is also completely and totally untrue'.[155]

The Hutton Inquiry heard compelling evidence that there was actually a great deal of disquiet. One senior member of the Defence Intelligence Staff, Dr Brian Jones, had taken the memorable step of writing to management to express his concern.[156]

Lord Hutton took none of this evidence into account when he published his conclusions at the start of 2004. He bizarrely accepted the contention that John Scarlett and his JIC were free from political pressure. He did so despite the fact that this thesis was contradicted by evidence to his inquiry – for instance, by a last-minute email from the prime minister's chief of staff on 19 September 2002 asking for a redraft because the prime minister had 'a bit of a problem' with a passage in the current draft, which was about to be cleared for publication.

In paragraph 228(7), Hutton speculated about whether Downing Street's desire to have a dossier which was 'as strong as possible' might have 'subconsciously influenced Mr Scarlett and the other members of the JIC to make the wording of

---

155 *Hansard*, House of Commons Debates, 4 June 2003, Col. 148.
156 See http://www.iraqinquirydigest.org/?p=4577.

the dossier somewhat stronger than it would have been if it had been contained in a normal JIC assessment'. However, he concluded:

> Although this possibility cannot be completely ruled out, I am satisfied that Mr Scarlett, the other members of the JIC, and the members of the assessment staff engaged in the drafting of the dossier were concerned to ensure that the contents of the dossier were consistent with the intelligence available to the JIC.

Three months before this was published, the Intelligence and Security Committee had shown that the contents of the dossier were *not* consistent with the intelligence available to the JIC at the time.

One other mystery concerns the Hutton Inquiry. Its purpose was to investigate the circumstances surrounding the death of Dr David Kelly. It acted as a replacement for a coroner's inquest. The judge concluded that Kelly had taken his own life by slashing the ulnar artery in his left wrist and swallowing a large number of Coproxamol painkiller tablets.[157]

However, mystery has continued to surround the case. Because Dr Kelly's death was not subject to a coroner's inquest, no evidence at the Hutton Inquiry was given under oath. A group of doctors, led by surgeon David Halpin and radiologist Stephen Frost, questioned whether Kelly could have died in

---

157 'Report of the Inquiry into the Circumstances Surrounding the Death of Dr David Kelly C.M.G. by Lord Hutton', 28 January 2004, HC 247.

the manner described by Lord Hutton. They said it was 'highly improbable' that Dr Kelly could have bled to death because the ulnar artery is too small.[158]

In 2007 Norman Baker, then a Liberal Democrat MP, published a book about the case in which he stated that the knife Kelly supposedly used had no fingerprints on it. He also noted a number of other oddities: Lord Hutton had not called the police officer in charge of the investigation into Dr Kelly's death, Chief Inspector Alan Young. Nor did he call the scientist's close friend, Mai Pedersen. Norman Baker said that she would have been able to tell Lord Hutton that Dr Kelly had damaged his right arm and was incapable of cutting steak, let alone cutting his left wrist.[159]

Lord Hutton himself later acknowledged that he had paid relatively little attention to the immediate train of events leading to David Kelly's death. Writing in the Inner Temple Yearbook 2004–2005 he observed: 'I thought that there would be little serious dispute as to the background facts [as reported in the press]. … I thought that unnecessary time could be taken up by cross-examination on matters which were not directly relevant.'

So key questions went unasked. Speaking in the House of Commons, Norman Baker accused Lord Hutton of failing 'to investigate conflicts of evidence when they were presented to him.'[160] In January 2010 journalist Miles Goslett revealed that

158 Letter: 'Our doubts about Dr Kelly's suicide', *Guardian*, 27 January 2004.
159 Norman Baker, 'Hutton was farcical, feeble and amateurish …', Mail Online, 25 January 2010.
160 *Hansard*, House of Commons Debates, 5 March 2010, Col 1189–90.

Hutton had secretly recommended that all medical reports relating to Kelly's death, plus photographs of his body, should be classified for seventy years.[161]

THE BUTLER INQUIRY

The fourth report set up in the wake of the Iraq invasion was chaired by Lord Butler, the former cabinet secretary. This inquiry, which had Sir John Chilcot as a member of the inquiry team, was launched just after the publication of the Hutton report. It was concerned with the government's use of intelligence material on Iraq's weapons of mass destruction. As such, it covered the same ground as the earlier Intelligence and Security Committee inquiry. It was mildly critical, while overall giving support to the government. It reported on 14 July 2004.[162]

Intellectually, the Butler Inquiry was something of a shambles. For instance, paragraph 464 of its report said:

> Strenuous efforts were made to ensure that no individual
> statements were made in the dossier which went beyond the
> judgements of the JIC. *But, in translating material from JIC*
> *assessments into the dossier, warnings were lost about the limited*
> *intelligence base on which some aspects of these assessments were*

---

161 'David Kelly post mortem to be kept secret for 70 years as doctors accuse Lord Hutton of concealing vital information', Mail Online, 25 January 2010. Part of this embargo was undone nine months later, when the government published the autopsy report.

162 news.bbc.co.uk/nol/shared/bsp/hi/pdfs/14_07_04_butler.pdf.

being made. The Government would have seen these warnings in the original JIC assessments and taken them into account in reading them. But the public, through reading the dossier, would not have known of them. The dossier did contain a chapter on the role of intelligence. *But the language in the dossier may have left with readers the impression that there was fuller and firmer intelligence behind the judgements than was the case: our view, having reviewed all of the material, is that judgements in the dossier went to (although not beyond) the outer limits of the intelligence available.* The Prime Minister's description, in his statement to the House of Commons on the day of publication of the dossier, of the picture painted by the intelligence services in the dossier as 'extensive, detailed and authoritative' may have reinforced this impression. [Author's emphasis]

That paragraph contradicts itself. Having said that the JIC assessments were not accurately reflected in the dossier, it goes on to say that 'judgements in the dossier' didn't go beyond 'the outer limits of the intelligence available'.[163]

The inquiry report went on to criticize the fact that the government presented the dossier to the public as authored by the Joint Intelligence Committee and it recommended that this method of presenting intelligence-based information should be avoided in future:

---

163 Yet the Butler report stated that there was 'a stronger assessment in the dossier in relation to Iraqi chemical weapons production than was justified by the available Intelligence'. Butler Review, 2004, paragraph 577, p. 139.

We conclude, with the benefit of hindsight, that making public that the JIC had authorship of the dossier was a mistaken
judgement, though we do not criticize the JIC for taking responsibility for clearance of the intelligence content of the document.
However, in the particular circumstances, the publication of
such a document in the name and with the authority of the
JIC had the result that more weight was placed on the intelli-
gence than it could bear. The consequence also was to put the
JIC and its Chairman into an area of public controversy and
arrangements must be made for the future which avoid putting the JIC and its Chairman in a similar position. [Author's
emphasis]

Having written this, the report went on to exempt JIC Chairman John Scarlett, who by then had been appointed head of MI6,
from any blame:

In reaching these conclusions, we realize that our conclusions
may provoke calls for the current Chairman of the JIC, Mr
Scarlett, to withdraw from his appointment as the next Chief
of SIS. We greatly hope that he will not do so. We have a high
regard for his abilities and his record. Once the Government
had decided to produce a dossier based on intelligence, he and
the JIC took on ownership of it with the excellent motive of
ensuring that everything it said was consistent with JIC judgements. We have said above that it was a mistaken judgement for
the dossier to be so closely associated with the JIC but it was

a collective one for which the Chairman of the JIC should not
bear personal responsibility.

As time passed Lord Butler has been more forthright about
the government's misuse of intelligence. He has spoken in the
House of Lords on at least two occasions about the inquiry he
headed, and on both occasions he went further in his criticism
of the Blair government.

Speaking in the House of Lords on 7 September 2004 he
accused the September dossier of failing to make clear that
'the intelligence underlying those conclusions was very thin, even
though the JIC assessments had been quite clear about that'.[164] As
we have seen, just over two years later, on 22 February 2007, he
accused Tony Blair of being 'disingenuous' about Iraq's weapons
of mass destruction. It is worth repeating once more what he said:

> The United Kingdom intelligence community told him on
> 23 August 2002 that, 'we ... know little about Iraq's chemical and
> biological weapons work since late 1988'. The Prime Minister
> did not tell us that. Indeed, he told Parliament only just over a
> month later that the picture painted by our intelligence services
> was 'extensive, detailed and authoritative'. Those words could
> simply not have been justified by the material that the intelli-
> gence community provided to him.[165]

Here Lord Butler is effectively accusing Tony Blair of lying.

---

164 Lords *Hansard*, 7 September 2004, Col 463.
165 Lords *Hansard*, 22 February 2007, Col 1231.

Had he made these remarks in his inquiry report, the prime minister would surely have been obliged to resign.

ROBIN COOK

In the Commons debate on the Butler report on 20 July 2004, Robin Cook said:

> I saw many intelligence assessments when I was at the Foreign Office. Doubt and intelligence assessments go hand in hand; doubt is in the nature of intelligence work. One is trying to guess the secrets that somebody is trying to keep, so it inevitably follows that one is trying to carry out a task even worse than that of the Israelites: to make bricks out of straws in the wind. To be fair to the agencies, they were always absolutely frank about the limitations of their knowledge. That is why I was frankly astonished by the September dossier, which bore no relation in tone to any of the intelligence assessments that I saw. It was one-sided, dogmatic and unqualified.[166]

Yet Cook, as leader of the House at the time, lent his name to this 'one-sided, dogmatic and unqualified' document for the next six months by staying in the cabinet. Had he resigned in September 2002, and described the dossier in such damning terms it might have been impossible for the prime minister to take Britain to war.

---

166 *Hansard*, House of Commons Debates, 20 July 2004, Col 227.

THE CHILCOT INQUIRY BEGINS

The Chilcot Inquiry into the Iraq War was not announced until nearly five years after Butler reported. On 15 June 2009, Prime Minister Gordon Brown set up his Iraq inquiry team, which would consist of four knights and a baroness – visible signs that they had been approved by the Establishment. Its chairman, Sir John Chilcot, had been permanent secretary at the Northern Ireland Office and as a former member of the Butler Inquiry he had a head start over all his colleagues in studying intelligence and policy in the run-up to the war.

The inquiry team also included Sir Lawrence Freedman, a distinguished military historian and analyst, who had written the official history of the Falklands campaign. His memorandum on five tests for military intervention had been used by Tony Blair in the preparation of his speech in Chicago in 1999 on 'humanitarian intervention', although he had later described the Bush administration's conduct of the war as 'dysfunctional'.[167]

Sir Martin Gilbert, best known for the official biography of Winston Churchill, was another historian on the team. In 2004 he had compared Blair and Bush to Churchill and Roosevelt. This article was frequently quoted when he joined the inquiry but, in fairness, the comparison was qualified rather than definitive: 'they may well, with the passage of time and the opening of the archives, join the ranks of Roosevelt and Churchill. Their societies are too divided today and many of their achievements may

---

167 'Who is on the Iraq War Inquiry Committee?', *Guardian*, 24 November 2009, www.theguardian.com/uk/2009/nov/24/chilcot-inquiry-iraq-committee.

be in the future: when Iraq has a stable democracy, with al-Qaeda neutralized and when Israel and the Palestinian Authority are independent democracies, living side by side in constructive economic co-operation.'[168] Sadly, Sir Martin died in February 2015 with none of those conditions fulfilled and the inquiry report far from publication.

Sir Roderic Lyne was a former ambassador to Russia and to the UN in Geneva, and had also served in the private office of John Major when he was prime minister, with responsibilities for defence and foreign policy. Baroness Prashar made up the panel. A cross-bencher with a string of public service and charitable appointments, none directly relevant to Iraq, she was the current chair of the Judicial Appointments Commission.[169] Apart from Chilcot himself, the inquiry members had no recent knowledge of Iraq and no experience of extracting evidence from witnesses. None had any legal expertise or recent first-hand military experience.

Sir John Chilcot opened the inquiry on 30 July 2009 with a lengthy statement at a news conference. He confirmed that it would cover the period from summer 2001 to the end of July 2009. 'We will therefore be considering the UK's involvement in Iraq, including the way decisions were made and actions taken, to establish as accurately as possible what happened and to identify the lessons learned.'[170]

---

168 'Statesmen for These Times', *Observer*, 26 December 2004.
169 For the strongest parliamentary criticism of the appointees see Lynne Jones, *Hansard*, House of Commons Debates, 24 June 2009, Col 874.
170 Transcript of opening press conference, www.iraqinquiry.org.uk/transcripts/opening.aspx.

Chilcot sanctioned that 'the inquiry is not a court of law and nobody is on trial', but then almost immediately promised that 'the committee will not shy away from making criticism. If we find that mistakes were made, that there were issues which could have been dealt with better, we will say so frankly.'

The term 'mistakes' was suggestive, since it carried the assumption that everyone concerned had acted in good faith and to the best of their abilities. Joe Murphy of the *Evening Standard* asked Chilcot if he agreed with Tony Blair's statement after the Butler Inquiry that 'the question of good faith could be parked; it was over'. Chilcot's reply was bumbling:

> I said in my statement that among many things the legality of the law would be one of the issues we shall need to examine. In other words, we start not with a blank sheet because history has happened and many of the facts are out, but the judgements about the facts, and many of the facts that have yet to emerge, those are for us to do from scratch.

However, he was much clearer in a reply to Bénédicte Paviot of France 24: 'If we find that people fell short in their duty, made mistakes, acted wrongly, we shall most certainly say so and say so clearly.'

TEN

IS TONY BLAIR A WAR CRIMINAL?

'To initiate a war of aggression, therefore, is not only an international crime; it is the supreme international crime differing only from other war crimes in that it contains within itself the accumulated evil of the whole.'

THE NUREMBERG TRIBUNAL, 1946[171]

Let's throw our minds back and remember what Britain was like on the eve of war with Iraq in the early months of 2003. It was a prosperous country, halfway through a sustained economic boom.

The Conservatives, under their short-lived leader Iain Duncan Smith, were a laughing stock. One man dominated the political landscape – Tony Blair. Only forty-nine years old, he had led

---

171 30 September 1946, http://avalon.law.yale.edu/imt/09-30-46.asp.

his New Labour Party to its second consecutive general election victory, winning another thumping majority on the back of his record landslide of 1997.

Mr Blair claimed to offer a new synthesis between market and state, between hard-headed economics and social compassion, between the individual and society. He rejected what he viewed as the narrow dogmatism of Left and Right. The British people liked this vision: very few British prime ministers had ever been so popular for so long.

On foreign policy, Tony Blair expressed idealism. He was convinced that advanced countries like Britain should deploy their economic and political strength to make the world a better place. He had set out this vision of humanitarian intervention in a famous speech in Chicago in 1999.[172]

The Chicago speech was made in the context of the NATO war over Kosovo to protect the population from Serbian ethnic cleansing. The following year, the prime minister authorized a mission to Sierra Leone, which changed the course of a particularly brutal civil war in the west African state.

Tony Blair had recently ordered what looked at the time to have been a successful military intervention in Afghanistan. Blair, it seemed, could do no wrong. It is little surprise that George

---

172 Looking back a decade later, Blair stressed: 'I set out what I described as a doctrine of international community that sought to justify intervention, including if necessary military intervention, not only when a nation's interests are directly engaged; but also where there exists a humanitarian crisis or gross oppression of a civilian population. It was a speech that argued strongly for an active and engaged foreign policy, not a reactive or isolationist one: better to intervene than to leave well alone. Be bold, adventurous even in what we can achieve.' Tony Blair, 'Speech to Chicago Council on Global Affairs', 23 April 2009.

W. Bush found the British prime minister very easy to persuade when it came to Iraq.

WAS BLAIR COMMITTED TO WAR FROM THE START?

In Chapter 6 I told the story of how Tony Blair persuaded George W. Bush to seek authorization from the United Nations for the war. I speculated that this achievement alone meant that had Tony Blair fallen under the proverbial bus in the autumn of 2002, he might now be hailed as one of our greatest prime ministers.

In this chapter I examine the sincerity of Tony Blair's commitment to the United Nations route. I will show that there are strong grounds for believing that regime change was the outcome agreed between George Bush and Tony Blair from at least a year before the invasion, and that leaving Saddam Hussein in power, with or without weapons of mass destruction, was never going to be tolerated in Washington.

Remember, regime change in Iraq had been the official policy of the US since October 1998, when President Clinton signed the Iraq Liberation Act into law. This act stated that it was 'the policy of the United States to support efforts to remove the regime headed by Saddam Hussein from power in Iraq' and offered military support to opposition groups in Iraq to bring this about.[173] By early 2002, President Bush had decided to take direct military action against Iraq to put this established policy into effect.

---

173 www.congress.gov/bill/105th-congress/house-bill/4655/text.

Aware of this, the Blair government set about persuading the Bush administration that, if the US wanted support from Britain, the matter would best be addressed through the United Nations.

To that end, Tony Blair's foreign policy adviser Sir David Manning met President Bush's National Security adviser Condoleezza Rice in March 2002. Sir David afterwards sent a memo to the prime minister reporting on the meeting, which included the following:

> I said [to Condoleezza Rice] that you would not budge in your support for regime change but you had to manage a press, a Parliament and a public opinion that was very different than anything in the States. And you would not budge either on your insistence that, if we pursued regime change, it must be very carefully done, and produce the right result.[174]

On the face of it, this memo proves that in March 2002 the Bush administration was given an assurance that Tony Blair was unflinching in his commitment to regime change in Iraq, and not merely to its disarmament in accordance with Security Council resolutions, as he told the British public at the time and for the next year.[175]

The impression that Tony Blair was committed to regime change from March 2002 is reinforced by another memo, this

---

174 warisacrime.org/downloads/manning020314.pdf.
175 For example, on 25 February 2003 Tony Blair told the House of Commons: 'I detest his [Saddam Hussein's] regime … but even now, he could save it by complying with the UN's demand. Even now, we are prepared to go the extra step to achieve disarmament peacefully.'

one from Sir Christopher Meyer, the British ambassador in Washington, to Sir David Manning himself. This reported on a conversation with Paul Wolfowitz, the US deputy defense secretary, on 17 March 2002. The next day, Sir Christopher wrote to Sir David, as follows:

> I opened by sticking very closely to the script that you used with Condi Rice. We backed regime change, but the plan had to be clever and failure was not an option. It would be a tough sell for us domestically, and probably tougher elsewhere in Europe. The US could go it alone if it wanted to. But if it wanted to act with partners, there would have to be a strategy for building support for military action against Saddam. I then went through the need to wrongfoot Saddam on the inspectors ...[176]

Later, in November 2005, Sir Christopher published an account of his time in Washington as British ambassador in a book called *DC Confidential*. In it, he wrote: 'By this stage, Tony Blair had already taken the decision to support regime change, though he was discreet about saying so in public.'[177]

Neither Sir David Manning nor Tony Blair was questioned about the contents of the offending memos when they gave evidence to the Chilcot Inquiry. However, when asked at the inquiry on 29 January 2010 whether he had regarded the regime change as a 'valid objective for the government's policy', Tony Blair's

---

176 warisacrime.org/downloads/meyer020318.pdf.

177 C. Meyer, *DC Confidential*, Phoenix, 2005, p. 241. He was writing of the time in early April 2002, when Tony Blair met George Bush at his ranch in Crawford, Texas.

response was unequivocal: 'The absolutely key issue was the WMD issue,' he said.[178]

This assertion has been partially undermined by several extracts from Alastair Campbell's diaries. These add weight to the view that Tony Blair had made up his mind in favour of regime change by April 2002.

> *2 April 2002:*
>
> We discussed whether the central aim was WMD or regime change ... TB felt it was regime change in part because of WMD but more broadly because of the threat to the region and the world.

> *31 August 2002:*
>
> Blair was a lot steelier than when we went on holiday. Clear that getting Saddam was the right thing to do.

> *23 September 2002:*
>
> TB ... really believed in getting rid of bad people like Saddam.[179]

WRONGFOOTING SADDAM

But how was international support for regime change going to be mobilized? According to Sir Christopher Meyer, the plan was

---

178 www.iraqinquiry.org.uk/media/45139/20100129-blair-final.pdf.
179 A. Campbell, *The Alastair Campbell Diaries*, Vol. 4, Arrow, 2013, pp. 198, 288, 307.

to 'wrongfoot Saddam on the inspectors'. By this he may have meant that an attempt would be made to persuade the Security Council to pass a resolution prescribing an inspection regime that was so unpalatable to Saddam Hussein that he would refuse to readmit inspectors.

In that event, there would have been a good chance of persuading the Security Council to authorize military action against Iraq ostensibly to disarm Iraq, but in the process the regime of Saddam Hussein would be brought down. A leaked Cabinet Office paper dated 21 June 2002 speculated about exactly this possibility:

> It is just possible that an ultimatum could be cast in terms which Saddam would reject (because he is unwilling to accept unfettered access) and which would not be regarded as unreasonable by the international community. However, failing that (or an Iraqi attack) we would be most unlikely to achieve a legal base for military action by January 2003.[180]

And according to the leaked minutes of a high-powered meeting in Downing Street on 23 July 2002, Tony Blair was of the same mind: '… it would make a big difference politically and legally', he said, 'if Saddam refused to allow in the UN inspectors … If the political context were right, people would support regime change.'[181]

The disarmament of Iraq by peaceful means required UN

---

180 warisacrime.org/node/189.
181 warisacrime.org/downloads/dsmemo.pdf.

inspectors being on the ground in Iraq. Yet, here the prime minister is expressing the hope that Saddam Hussein would refuse to allow UN inspectors in. Those were not the words of someone who was dedicated to securing the disarmament of Iraq by peaceful means, as he regularly told the British public.

In furtherance of this strategy of wrongfooting Saddam, the US and Britain attempted to get the Security Council to pass a resolution which laid down conditions which Iraq couldn't possibly accept, while clearly authorizing military action in that event without further recourse to the council.

On 2 October 2002 the US and Britain proposed a draft resolution, geared to achieve these objectives.[182] So, if this draft had been approved by the Security Council, US and British forces would have been authorized to enter Iraq on the pretext of being part of the inspection process. And if Iraq refused to allow the execution of these provisions, the draft resolution authorized member states 'to use all necessary means to restore international peace and security in the area'.

In other words, if Saddam Hussein refused to accept inspectors on these terms, the US and Britain would have been unambiguously authorized by the Security Council to take military action against

---

182 www.casi.org.uk/info/usukdraftscro21002.html. It contained the following provisions (paragraph 5):

- 'any permanent member of the Security Council may request to be represented on any inspection team with the same rights and protections accorded other members of the team';
- 'teams shall be accompanied at their bases by sufficient UN security forces to protect them';
- '[teams] shall have the right to declare for the purpose of this resolution no-fly/no-drive zones, exclusion zones, and/or ground and air transit corridors (which shall be enforced by UN security forces or by member states)'.

Iraq forthwith. In this event, there would have been no argument about the 'legality' of military action. It would, indeed, have made 'a big difference politically and legally', in the prime minister's words.

But the US and Britain didn't get their way: with France taking the lead, the special rights afforded to permanent members of the council in the inspection process were removed, together with any suggestion that they could put forces on the ground in Iraq as part of the inspection process. The explicit authorization of the use of force, without a further Security Council resolution, was deleted. The Security Council eventually passed the amended resolution on 8 November 2002 as Resolution 1441.

France was interested in making practical arrangements for verifying the disarmament of Iraq by inspection. By contrast, the US and Britain seemed to have been more interested in putting conditions on inspection which Iraq wouldn't accept, so that inspectors would never enter Iraq again, and getting Security Council authorization for military action in the event of Iraq's refusal to admit inspectors.

But, thanks to France, Germany and Russia, Resolution 1441 was acceptable to Iraq. It then allowed inspectors in, while repeating that it had no 'weapons of mass destruction'. The attempt to 'wrongfoot Saddam on the inspectors' had failed. The US and Britain were denied immediate Security Council authorization for military action.

UN inspectors operating under Resolution 1441 worked in Iraq from 27 November 2002 until 18 March 2003, when their work was terminated by impending US/UK military action to bring about regime change, embarked upon without Security Council authorization.

INSPECTORS KEPT OUT OF IRAQ

In December 1998, UN weapons inspectors were withdrawn from Iraq for their own safety at the request of President Clinton, because the US and UK were about to launch Operation Desert Fox, a three-day bombing campaign. On 16 September 2002 Iraq stated its willingness to admit UN weapons inspectors, having refused to do so in the intervening four years. The reaction to this by the US and the UK suggests that disarmament by inspection was not uppermost in their minds.

Up to then, the US and UK had been clamouring for Iraq to do so, but, when Iraq said 'yes', they refused to take 'yes' for an answer. Other members of the Security Council, for example, France and Russia, were in favour of inspection beginning right away, but the United States opposed this.

On 19 September 2002 US Secretary of State Colin Powell gave evidence to the House of Representatives International Relations Committee and was asked what the administration would do 'if, within the Security Council, some of the permanent representatives, France, Russia, China, would insist on proceeding with inspections under the current existing UN regime'. He replied: 'We would oppose it. We would oppose it ... And if somebody tried to move the team in now, we would find ways to thwart that.'[183] Or he may simply have hoped that any demand for the readmission of inspectors would be unacceptable to Saddam.

---

183 commdocs.house.gov/committees/intlrel/hfa81814.000/hfa81814_0.HTM.

Remember that around this time the British government published its dossier on Iraq's weapons of mass destruction and, in presenting it to Parliament on 24 September 2002, the prime minister warned the British public of a growing danger from these weapons.

Despite this allegedly growing threat, at the same time Tony Blair's allies in Washington were actively preventing UN inspectors from re-entering Iraq. Stopping inspectors entering Iraq in September 2002 made little sense if the prime minister's objective was the disarmament of Iraq by inspection. It made no sense at all if the danger from Iraq's proscribed weapons was growing, since the presence of inspectors on the ground would obviously render the production and deployment of proscribed weapons more difficult.

So what were the US and the UK up to in blocking inspection in September 2002? The answer is that this was part of the plan to 'wrongfoot Saddam on the inspectors'. In other words, they hoped to persuade the Security Council to pass a tough resolution prescribing an inspection regime that was so unpalatable to Saddam Hussein that he would refuse to allow inspectors in.

WHY NO NEW JIC ASSESSMENT?

Given the inspectors' failure by early 2003 to uncover evidence that Iraq still possessed proscribed weapons, having examined many sites deemed suspect by the United States and Britain, including 'every single site' mentioned in the government's dossier, was there not a case for looking at the intelligence again? The inquiry headed by Lord Butler thought so – its report published in July 2004 expressed 'surprise that policy-makers and the intelligence community did not, as the generally negative results of UNMOVIC inspections became increasingly apparent, re-evaluate in early-2003 the quality of the intelligence'.[184]

Moreover, so did Sir David Omand, who held the post of security and intelligence co-ordinator in the Cabinet Office from June 2002 until April 2005. Giving evidence to the Chilcot Inquiry on 20 January 2010, he expressed regret that:

> We didn't in the JIC [Joint Intelligence Committee] step back in January [2003] at the time of the first report, the interim report, of the inspectors and say, 'Let's look again at all our intelligence and all of our inferences against what has been found on the ground.'[185]

But he added: 'It wasn't asked for, it wouldn't have been welcome.' Indeed, a new assessment in February/March 2003 expressing doubt about Iraq's possession of proscribed weapons would have undermined the case for invasion and regime change. That would not have been welcome in Downing Street. The JIC does not need to be asked: it has carte blanche to produce assessments whenever it judges appropriate. The phrase 'it wouldn't have been welcome' is further evidence that the JIC may have been subject to political constraints.

---

184 news.bbc.co.uk/nol/shared/bsp/hi/pdfs/14_07_04_butler.pdf, paragraph 472.
185 www.iraqinquiry.org.uk/media/44187/20100120pm-omand-final.pdf.

BLAIR'S ADDRESS TO THE NATION

On 20 March 2003, as British forces went into action in Iraq, the prime minister addressed the nation. In his address he justified his decision to take military action in the following terms:

> For twelve years, the world tried to disarm Saddam ... UN weapons inspectors say vast amounts of chemical and biological poisons, such as anthrax, VX nerve agent, and mustard gas remain unaccounted for in Iraq.
>
> So our choice is clear: back down and leave Saddam hugely strengthened; or proceed to disarm him by force. Retreat might give us a moment of respite but years of repentance at our weakness would I believe follow.[186]

But, if one was committed to disarmament rather than regime change, the alternative to military action in March 2003 was not 'to back down and leave Saddam hugely strengthened': it was, rather, to *continue inspections*.

Even if one believed that Iraq had an arsenal of proscribed weapons and was manufacturing more, it wasn't necessary to invade Iraq, and overthrow the regime, in order to disarm it. Inspection could have continued indefinitely and it stands to reason that, while inspection and other forms of surveillance were going on, Saddam Hussein's ability to manufacture agents and weapons and deploy them, assuming he had a mind to, would be greatly inhibited.

---

186 news.bbc.co.uk/1/hi/uk_politics/2870581.stm.

On 18 March 2003, the UN inspectors were once again withdrawn from Iraq for their own safety in anticipation of US/UK military action against Iraq, this time to remove Saddam Hussein from power. The action began the next day without authorization from the Security Council.

This date was not determined by the progress or otherwise of the ongoing weapons inspections. It was not triggered by the inspectors reporting that they couldn't do any more useful work, because, for example, they were being obstructed by the Iraqi regime. On the contrary, the inspectors were anxious to have more time to complete their mission.

No, the date was determined by the US military timetable, to which the UK had assented. The Bush administration decided that the US forces already in the region in preparation for the invasion of Iraq could not be held back any longer. The UK had already asked the US for a week's delay, which was granted. A factor in refusing a further delay was the reluctance on the part of the US military to fight a war during the hot Iraqi summer.

So, on 19 March 2003, the possibility of a peaceful UN route of disarmament by inspection was aborted by the United States and Britain without the consent of the Security Council. The United States and Britain alone made the decision to terminate disarmament by inspection, which was proceeding relatively unhindered, and to replace it with disarmament by military force.

LOOKING INSIDE THE MIND OF TONY BLAIR

Iraq is frequently described as Blair's war and reasonably so. The one consistent theme of his conduct is his enthusiasm, bordering on obsession, for Britain to join the Iraq War.

Other modern British prime ministers might have hesitated before committing Britain to George Bush's war for regime change.[187] They might have had moral doubts about sending men to die in a war which was unnecessary and unlawful. They might have had practical doubts about the consequences of the war and the scale of commitments required to secure a successful aftermath. They might have had political doubts about the impact of the war on their leadership. They might, too, have tried to limit Britain's commitment to the war and the subsequent occupation. Blair, however, always went for the maximum commitment.

Other prime ministers might have reached for some excuse to avoid or postpone commitment to Bush's war. The intelligence is uncertain ... the lawyers are against it ... Afghanistan is unfinished business ... there is no plan for the aftermath ... But Blair used none of these arguments within his own government, let alone to George W. Bush. When the intelligence was uncertain, when the legal advice went the wrong way, he asked for them to be adjusted. Blair never once looked for any way out of the war.

---

187 With the possible exception of Anthony Eden, who took Britain into the Suez War on a cocktail of stimulant and painkilling drugs which has since been banned (see 'Eden "was on purple hearts during Suez crisis"', *Independent*, 4 November 2006). Although Eden's war was far less destructive than Blair's, it ended his political career and he became a forgotten man for the remaining twenty years of his life. Politicians in the 1950s still had to pay a price for error and failure.

Tony Blair never thought his predecessors had anything to teach him – except negatively. His mental calendar began with his ascent to his party's leadership. Characteristically, Blair never had any conversation with John Major about Iraq,[188] even though he had actually taken Britain into a successful war against Saddam Hussein in 1991. Blair appears to have had no curiosity about why the allies had stopped short of regime change in the first Gulf War.

Even allowing for Blair's 'personal myth' as a prime minister like no other there is still a central mystery about the depth of his commitment to the Iraq War. He must have known that he was never going to be more than a supporting actor in the drama, with no real influence on the plot. Why was he so desperate to get the role of the hero's best friend?

Blair's commitment becomes explicable only in terms of his conception of the Anglo-American relationship. Other prime ministers saw this as a means to accomplish British goals. Blair clearly saw it as an end in itself – and one which required total support for any major American initiative.

ON BLAIR'S ALLEGED WAR CRIMES

After the Second World War, the victors established an International Military Tribunal at Nuremberg to try leading Nazis. Article 6 of the tribunal's constitution specified the crimes falling

---

188 Personal knowledge.

within its jurisdiction. First and foremost was the 'planning, preparation, initiation or waging of a war of aggression'.[189]

During the trials, Justice Robert H. Jackson, the United States chief prosecutor, declared a war of aggression to be the 'supreme' international crime. He said:

> To initiate a war of aggression, therefore, is not only an international crime; it is the supreme international crime differing only from other war crimes in that it contains within itself the accumulated evil of the whole.[190]

As a prime mover in the invasion of Iraq, which was not a war of self-defence against Iraqi aggression and was not authorized by the Security Council, Tony Blair could reasonably be accused of committing the 'supreme' international crime, and so too could George Bush.

Noam Chomsky told the BBC in May 2004 that if George Bush were to be judged by the standards of the Nuremberg Tribunal for invading Iraq, he'd be hanged – and so would every single American president since World War II, including Jimmy Carter.[191]

Back in the real world, where victors establish tribunals to try the vanquished, there was no court in which either Bush or Blair could be tried for the crime of aggression in 2003 or subsequently.

The only court which could conceivably have tried Tony Blair was the International Criminal Court (ICC). By the time of the

189 avalon.law.yale.edu/imt/imtconst.asp#art6.
190 30 September 1946, http://avalon.law.yale.edu/imt/09-30-46.asp.
191 news.bbc.co.uk/1/hi/programmes/newsnight/3732345.stm.

invasion, the UK was a party to the ICC, which came into operation on 1 July 2002. In principle, individuals, not excluding heads of state, could be tried for genocide, war crimes or crimes against humanity, as defined in the ICC's Rome Statute.

But, as Lord Goldsmith pointed out in his legal advice to Tony Blair on 7 March 2003, the court had 'no jurisdiction over the crime of aggression and could therefore not entertain a case concerning the lawfulness of any military action'.[192]

In this respect, the attorney general's advice was non-controversial and proved to be correct – in leading the UK to war against Iraq, Tony Blair had nothing to worry about from the ICC. (The ICC's Rome Statute has been amended since to introduce a crime of aggression, but time will tell whether individuals will ever be prosecuted.)

In his legal advice on 7 March 2003, Lord Goldsmith also pointed out: 'The ICC will however have jurisdiction to examine whether any military campaign has been conducted in accordance with international humanitarian law.' This is so because, by becoming a state party to the ICC, the UK accepted its jurisdiction over genocide, war crimes and crimes against humanity committed not just in the UK but also by UK nationals anywhere in the world. As a result, British servicemen could be prosecuted by the ICC for offences committed in Iraq – such as the abuse of civilians – and so could officers in their chain of command for ordering the abuse or allowing it to happen.

In May 2014, the ICC received a submission on this issue

---

192 www.theguardian.com/politics/2005/apr/28/election2005.uk.

which went so far as to name Geoff Hoon, the former defence secretary, and the former defence minister Adam Ingram.[193] The ICC prosecutor has agreed to 'conduct a preliminary examination' in order to 'determine whether there is a reasonable basis to proceed with an investigation'.[194]

The latter is very unlikely since the exercise of ICC jurisdiction comes into play only if domestic authorities fail to carry out proper investigations and, if appropriate, prosecutions – and it is inconceivable that the British government will fail to do that.

---

193 www.independent.co.uk/news/uk/politics/icc-will-investigate-abuse-by-uk-troops-in-iraq-9364931.html.

194 www.icc-cpi.int/en_menus/icc/press%20and%20media/press%20releases/Pages/otp-statement-iraq-13-05-2014.aspx.

CONCLUSION

'... ISIL is a direct outgrowth of al-Qaeda in Iraq that grew out of our invasion. Which is an example of unintended consequences. Which is why we should generally aim before we shoot.'

BARACK OBAMA, 16 MARCH 2015[195]

Some years ago, Britain's prime minister took this country into an unlawful and unprofitable war in the Middle East, and misled its Parliament and people about its purpose and its origins.

Anthony Eden's error at Suez brought swift political punishment. He was ejected from office and became a forgotten man for the remaining twenty years of his life. Suez also produced a major reappraisal of British policy and Britain's role in the world.

---

195 Interview with Vice News, https://www.youtube.com/watch?v=2a01Rg2g2Z8.

Tony Blair's errors in Iraq were far more calamitous for Britain, and Iraq, and the world.

The Iraq War, which he not only joined but encouraged, cost our country the lives of 179 soldiers and thousands more permanently wounded, physically and mentally. Financially, it cost at least £10 billion.[196] It increased the terrorist threat to Britain. The loss of life in Iraq is beyond calculation, and the country is no longer a functioning state. The war and the occupation led to the renaissance of al-Qaeda, the emergence of ISIS and the destabilization of large parts of the Middle East.

Yet Tony Blair won the 2005 general election comfortably. When he stepped down as prime minister in 2007 after ten years in power, internal party intrigue and not Iraq was the cause (though the war had left him much weaker). His successor, Gordon Brown, had voted for the Iraq War.

David Cameron, who became prime minister after the 2010 general election, was another supporter of the Iraq invasion. He was, furthermore, one of Tony Blair's keenest admirers, at one stage boasting that he was the 'heir to Blair'. As prime minister, David Cameron maintained Tony Blair's habit of attacking Muslim countries. During the Cameron premiership Britain has engaged in combat in Afghanistan (a conflict he inherited from Tony Blair and Gordon Brown), Libya, Iraq and Syria.

Meanwhile the opponents of the Iraq War are marginalized. Although Jeremy Corbyn, who voted against the invasion, was

---

196 A. L. Johnson (ed.), *Wars in Peace: British Military Operations Since 1991*, RUSI Publications, 2014. See also: 'UK Military Operations Since Cold War Have Cost £34bn, Says Study', *Guardian*, 23 April 2014, http://www. theguardian.com/world/2014/apr/23/uk-military-operations-costs.

elected leader of the Labour Party after Ed Miliband's resignation in 2015, he is plotted against by frontbench colleagues, and has found it impossible to gain a fair hearing in the mainstream media.

This brings us to a paradox. Thirteen years after the Iraq invasion the British neoconservatives are still in charge. Far from being discredited by the calamity of Iraq, they are stronger than ever and occupy key positions of influence at the inner core of the David Cameron government.

They appear to have learnt only one thing from Iraq: that voters, in both Britain and the United States, will no longer tolerate long wars without visible success which have long casualty lists. So the successor wars are largely conducted by remote means, with bombing, special forces and drones. Cynically, the neoconservatives think that domestic voters will not be concerned with the local civilian casualties which inevitably accompany such tactics.

However, exactly the same ideological disposition and view of the world prevails as it did when Tony Blair was prime minister. George Osborne and Michael Gove, the prime minister's two closest political allies, are both root and branch neoconservatives (for all that they are on opposite sides of the EU referendum debate). The prime minister himself seeks the foreign policy advice of Tony Blair.[197] There appears to be a new law in British politics: from whichever position you start out, British prime ministers end up turning into a version of Tony Blair.

---

197 Private information.

THE SURVIVAL OF NEOCONSERVATISM

What does neoconservatism mean? It is an especially confusing term because it has nothing whatever to do with conservatism as it is has been generally understood in Britain.[198] Despite its name it is at bottom a revolutionary doctrine, which supports ambitious programmes for the transformation of society – one reason why it was so attractive to a progressive leader like Tony Blair.

British conservatism is the opposite of revolutionary. Conservatives have a respect for history and tradition. This involves an understanding of the need for order; a grasp of the connection between the individual and society, mediated through institutions; a preference, all things considered, for keeping things as they are. This sort of conservative realizes that the future is defined by the past. They understand that our national institutions embody wisdoms and truths that are beyond the comprehension of individual minds, however clever.

As Edmund Burke, born in Ireland and – though by trade a writer and politician – the nearest thing we have to a conservative philosopher, remarked: 'I feel an insuperable reluctance in giving my hand to destroy any established institution of government upon a theory, however plausible it may be.'[199] By contrast neoconservatives tend to be contemptuous of tradition, which

---

198 The comparison with neoliberalism, another fashionable phrase, is useful. Neoliberalism is conceptually very hard to distinguish from classical liberalism as defined by John Stuart Mill or Adam Smith – that is, personal liberty and free markets. By contrast, neoconservatism is in conceptual terms the opposite of traditional conservatism.

199 *The Works of the Right Honourable Edmund Burke, Volume 2*, J. Dodsley, 1792, p. 335.

they see as prejudice. They are indifferent to history, which they understand as injustice.

Their indifference to historical continuity explains why Iraq was a classic neoconservative project. It was about tearing a society to pieces and starting all over again. Almost all of the mistakes of the Iraq invasion arose from the neoconservative belief that Western rationality, expressed through force, can reorder the world for the better. Sometimes, in the right circumstances, it can. At times, however, it can descend into naivety and is hard to distinguish from ignorance.

In the run-up to the Iraq War, Professor George Joffe, a Middle East expert at Cambridge University, was invited to meet Tony Blair to brief him on the likely consequences an occupying army would face. Joffe spoke of tribal and sectarian divisions, stressing that keeping order would be no easy matter. At the end of Joffe's exposition the prime minister looked across the table at the Cambridge expert and said, 'But he [Saddam] is evil, isn't he?' Joffe recalls:

> I have to say I was rather taken aback. Although that was no doubt the case, it didn't seem to me to correspond to the kind of issues you expected someone in his position to raise.[200]

The twin disasters of Iraq and Afghanistan have one essential point in common. They were founded in ignorance. British forces (in totally inadequate numbers) were ordered into areas

---

200 Conversation with the author, Cambridge 2005. See also http://www. theguardian.com/politics/2008/jan/21/iraq.iraq.

with a long history of resentment against foreign invaders. They as occupiers arrived knowing practically nothing of the people, the honour codes, the history or the tribes. Yet in both Iraq and Afghanistan the British government proposed far-reaching schemes of transformation. It is little wonder we were driven out.[201]

One of the most serious problems of the five-year delay in the publication of the Chilcot report is that ministers have continued to make the same mistakes that were made ahead of the Iraq invasion.

David Cameron's decision to attack Libya in 2011 was driven by the same naivety that drove the invasion of Iraq in 2003, or the intervention in Helmand Province from 2006. Cameron issued his orders in blithe ignorance of the culture, the traditional structures, the geography, the anthropology of Muammar Gaddafi's Libya. As in 2003, the pretext for war (in this case an alleged impending genocide) was exaggerated.[202] David Cameron had even less excuse than Tony Blair for getting it wrong because in

201 See R. Stewart and G. Knaus, *Can Intervention Work?*, W. W. Norton & Company, 2011. This book argues causes of crisis are not, as neoconservatives tend to assume, the result of structural flaws, blank 'ungoverned' space and helpless victims, but are instead specific to a particular place and time. Even the poorest, most fragile nations – such as post-war Kosovo or Afghanistan – are densely patterned with functioning local forms of security, administration and dispute resolution. These pre-dated the crisis, continue to support communities and will provide some of the solutions.

202 An investigation by the International Crisis Group found that there were 'grounds for questioning the more sensational reports that the [Libyan] regime was using its air force to slaughter demonstrators, let alone engaging in anything remotely warranting use of the term "genocide"' (*Popular Protest in North Africa and the Middle East (V): Making Sense of Libya, Crisis Group Middle East/North Africa*, Report No. 107, 6 June 2011, pp. 4–5. See also 'Amnesty Questions Claim that Gaddafi Ordered Rape as a Weapon of War', *Independent*, 23 June 2011.

the case of Libya the British prime minister ignored the advice of senior military adviser, General Sir David Richards.[203]

The intervention certainly succeeded in dislodging Gaddafi, just as Saddam was removed in 2003. As in 2003 the effect of regime change was to create an al-Qaeda presence which did not exist before. The intervention wrecked a functioning society. Without a strong leader, Libya has degenerated into anarchy, with large ungoverned spaces where al-Qaeda and (more recently) Islamic State can gain strength, terrorize the Libyan people and threaten the West.

THE SECRET INTELLIGENCE SERVICE AND IRAQ

The Chilcot Inquiry heard disturbing evidence that government inside Britain is failing. In the run-up to war Tony Blair was able to override the constitutional checks and balances which are supposed to prevent calamities such as Iraq or Afghanistan. To put the problem in another way, the British constitution was subverted by a charismatic leader who simply ignored established procedures.

Cabinet government ceased to operate as it should. Ministers did not see key documents.[204] Normal procedures ceased. One

---

203 Richards recalled that after telling a BBC interviewer he was wary of the legality of targeting Gaddafi, Cameron rebuked him with the words: 'You do the fighting, I'll do the talking' (see 'David Richards: "As a General, I Could Literally Change the Fortunes of a Nation"', *Huffington Post*, 9 October 2014).

204 As early as 2004 the Butler report expressed its concern that 'the informality and circumscribed character of the government's procedures which we saw in the context of policy making toward Iraq risks reducing the scope for

example concerns the failure to circulate the thirteen-page minute of advice from attorney general Lord Goldsmith on the legality of the war.[205]

Cabinet government was replaced by rule by coterie. Decision-making was confined to a small group of informal advisers around the prime minister. The two most powerful of these were Tony Blair's Director of Communications Alastair Campbell and his chief of staff Jonathan Powell.

This collapse in Whitehall integrity was especially worrisome when it came to the Secret Intelligence Service (SIS). This organization has in the past been respected for its scepticism and detachment. During the run-up to the Iraq War, however, intelligence chiefs and the Blairite political machine became unusually close. Meanwhile, SIS shockingly tolerated New Labour's use of secret intelligence as propaganda.[206]

The confusion of politics and intelligence started at the

---

informed political judgment' (*Review of Intelligence on Weapons of Mass Destruction*, 14 July 2004, p. 148, http://news.bbc.co.uk/nol/shared/bsp/hi/pdfs/14_07_04_butler.pdf). According to the *Independent* newspaper Lord Butler later told a Foreign Office seminar that 'a lot of very good official papers were prepared ... None was ever circulated to the Cabinet... I think that was deliberate, and it was a weakness of the machinery that underlay that particular decision' (*Independent*, 13 November 2013).

205 At least one member of the cabinet believed that the Ministerial Code had been breached by this action and wrote to the attorney general to complain. See Clare Short's evidence to the Iraq Inquiry of 2 February 2010, pp. 41–3 http://www.iraqinquiry.org.uk/media/44771/20100202am-short-final.pdf.

206 The Butler Inquiry went some distance towards conceding this when it concluded that 'the publication of such a document [the September 2002 dossier] in the name and with the authority of the JIC, had the result that more weight was placed on the intelligence than it could bear'. See pp. 113–14 https://fas.org/irp/world/uk/butler071404.PDF. Intelligence chiefs appear to have allowed Tony Blair repeatedly to misrepresent what they said in his public statements.

top with Richard Dearlove, who occupied the position of SIS chief often referred to as 'C'. Traditional SIS chiefs had been intimidating and distant figures, careful not to get involved in political battles.

By contrast Dearlove was sucked into the intimate circle around the prime minister. However, the JIC chief John Scarlett (in due course to replace Dearlove as head of MI6) developed a yet cosier connection with Number 10. On two occasions during the preparation of the September dossier Scarlett was present at a meeting chaired by Alastair Campbell.[207] Scarlett was in direct email contact with members of Campbell's press team. Comments on the intelligence dossier were invited from junior press officers.

It was as if the disciplines of press officer and spy became one. After the Iraq invasion, the former permanent secretary at the Ministry of Defence Michael Quinlan, wrote of an environment where 'there was a sense of all participants – ministers,

---

207　As the Hutton Inquiry recorded, 'On 5 September 2002 a meeting was held in the Cabinet Office to consider the preparation of the paper announced by the Prime Minister. The meeting was chaired by Mr Alastair Campbell and was attended by Sir David Manning, Mr John Scarlett, Mr Julian Miller and other officials from the Cabinet Office, the FCO and the MoD. A further meeting chaired by Mr Campbell was held in his office in 10 Downing Street on 9 September.' In his evidence to Hutton, Scarlett stressed in explanation that these meetings had been 'chaired by Alastair Campbell because they were unique – they were wholly and only concerned with those issues ['to finalize the arrangements for the format, the structure, and sort of taking forward the presentation of the government's assessment']. There was no discussion of intelligence issues, intelligence matters, intelligence at all, at that meeting or at those meetings so it was wholly appropriate, in my view, that they should be chaired by Alastair Campbell. It was not, in any sense of the term at all, an intelligence – neither of them were intelligence meetings' (*Report of the Inquiry into the Circumstances Surrounding the Death of Dr David Kelly C.M.G.*, 28 January 2004, p. 108).

civil servants, special policy advisors, public relations handlers – being treated as part of an undifferentiated resource'.[208] Press officers gained access to intelligence, while intelligence chiefs took on the role of press agents. Documents issued to the Hutton Inquiry show how John Scarlett found himself among a number of Downing Street aides clustered round the word-processor of a press spokesman called Godric Smith, drawing up a press release.[209] Vital Whitehall distinctions collapsed in the run-up to war. Spies, lawyers, press officers and ministers all became part of the same project.[210]

This propinquity between the intelligence and political establishments is a normal state of affairs in authoritarian states but unusual in democracies. Ahead of the invasion of Iraq, SIS could have used its special expertise and understanding to warn of the risks associated with an event as serious as the invasion of Iraq. Instead SIS allowed itself to become a willing and enthusiastic part of the government propaganda machine.

It is important to note that there is no serious evidence that SIS went to the lengths of inventing intelligence material that made the case for war (though it is arguable that it was too hasty in

---

208 Quoted in W. G. Runciman (ed.), *Hutton and Butler: Lifting the Lid on the Workings of Power*, British Academy/OUP, 2004, p. 128.

209 Godric Smith in evidence to Hutton Inquiry, 20 August 2003. The resulting press release was document CAB 1/56.

210 See the concluding paragraph of the Butler Review on this subject: 'We do not suggest that there is or should be an ideal or unchangeable system of collective Government, still less that procedures are in aggregate any less effective now than in earlier times. However, we are concerned that the informality and circumscribed character of the Government's procedures which we saw in the context of policy-making towards Iraq risks reducing the scope for informed collective political judgement.' Butler, op. cit., p. 148.

giving credibility to dubious claims under heavy pressure from ministers). However, SIS did place their own imprimatur on essentially political statements about intelligence material.

Again and again Tony Blair would make misleading or false assertions, either in Parliament or to the media, about Saddam Hussein's weapons of mass destruction. The prime minister's comments often exaggerated the threat posed by Saddam, and frequently cited, either explicitly or implicitly, the intelligence services as the source of his knowledge.[211]

I have found no evidence that either John Scarlett or Richard Dearlove ever complained that their work was being distorted by 10 Downing Street. This failure to complain meant that Scarlett and Dearlove were entering into a tacit conspiracy to deceive the British people ahead of the Iraq invasion.

Once again the lessons of Iraq have not been learned, as the case of Syria proves. Twelve years after the Iraq invasion another

---

211 For example, Tony Blair told MPs at the time of the second Iraqi 'dodgy' dossier in February 2003: 'we issued further information over the weekend about the infrastructure of concealment [in Iraq]. It is obviously difficult when we publish Intelligence reports, but I hope people have some sense of the integrity of our security services. They are not publishing this, or giving us this information and making it up. It is the intelligence that they are receiving and we are passing on to people.'

Here Tony Blair asserted in terms that British Intelligence was publishing 'the second dossier'. In fact, the full document had not been seen in advance by British Intelligence, let alone published by it. When questioned by the Foreign Affairs Committee, Alastair Campbell denied reports that he had apologized to intelligence chiefs after the provenance of the dossier, with its unattributed inclusion of work by a PhD student, was questioned. However, he later confirmed to the Intelligence and Security Committee that he had telephoned intelligence chiefs to apologize. (See the ISC report 'Iraqi Weapons of Mass Destruction – Intelligence and Assessments', Cm 5972, paragraph 132.) The original falsehood uttered by Tony Blair remains, remarkably enough, on the official Commons Record.

British prime minister, David Cameron, stood up in the Commons chamber to make the case for war. Just as Blair had done over Iraq, David Cameron leant heavily on 'our independent Joint Intelligence Committee, based on detailed analysis, updated daily and drawing on a wide range of open sources and intelligence' for his widely derided claim that Britain was able to rely on 70,000 Syrian rebel allies on the ground.[212] Cameron's invocation of the JIC seemed to repeat the mistake made by Tony Blair thirteen years earlier.[213]

The contrast between SIS and the domestic intelligence service MI5 is striking. For many years viewed by many in Whitehall as the inferior service and poor relation of SIS, MI5 emerges with its reputation enhanced from the Iraq tragedy. Rather than too eagerly help the government make the case for invasion of Iraq, MI5 soberly warned of the consequences. It predicted that a much graver al-Qaeda threat would result – a warning that ministers did not pass on to Parliament. For the last twelve years MI5 has devoted much of its energy and resources to dealing with the domestic consequences of SIS's foreign adventurism.

---

212 *Hansard*, House of Commons Debates, 2 December 2015, Col 333.
213 The Butler report had noted that the September dossier 'had put the JIC and its Chairman into an area of public controversy'. It recommended that 'arrangements must be made for the future which avoid putting the JIC and its Chairman in a similar position', http://news.bbc.co.uk/nol/shared/bsp/hi/pdfs/14_07_04_butler.pdf , p. 114.

THE SUMMING UP

The destruction of the Twin Towers in 2001 was a murderous assault on the United States which could not be ignored. But it was also the kind of opportunity which comes round only once in a century.

Global sympathy for the United States after 9/11 was colossal. Every important nation stretched out and extended a hand of friendship. The al-Qaeda atrocities gave the United States huge moral, emotional and political capital.

Take the example of Iran, an enemy of the US since the Islamic Revolution of 1979. There were candlelit vigils in Tehran, while the Iranian leadership made genuine offers of co-operation against al-Qaeda and the Taliban. Russia, meanwhile, wanted to talk to the United States constructively.

George W. Bush and his neoconservative advisers slammed the door in the faces of those who wanted to help. They responded to violence with violence, and pursued a policy which resulted in the invasion of Iraq.

In the decade after 9/11 the United States spent more than $3 trillion and squandered the lives of 7,000 American and allied soldiers. The consequences of these wars has been the destabilization of Iraq, the emergence of Islamic State, and a failed state in Afghanistan. Meanwhile, the reputation of America and its western allies has been gravely damaged by the rendition, torture and detention without trial of terror suspects, and other cases of western brutality, such as Abu Ghraib.

Bin Laden's strike on the Twin Towers drew the US into

a series of unprofitable wars which multiplied the power and influence of al-Qaeda and its successors and magnified the relative decline of the United States. Rather than hold back the United States, Tony Blair's Britain became the international cheerleader for war.

So let's try a mental experiment. Let's assume that the United States, supported by the United Kingdom, did not resolve to invade Iraq in early 2003. What would have happened if there had been no war against Saddam Hussein?

Of course there can never be a definitive answer to this hypothetical question. But it is hard to imagine that the Middle East and the world would be in a worse state than it is now, in consequence of the war. Would Iraq have collapsed as a state? Would terrorists even more barbaric than al-Qaeda now occupy large territories and victimize their populations? Would thousands of Iraqis have died needlessly and prematurely? Would the Middle East now be in flames leaving untold numbers of its people seeking refuge from it in Europe?

Tony Blair helped to promote the greatest calamity of the twenty-first century so far. He insisted that Britain should be part of it. And even now he still thinks that he was right to act as he did.

THE IMPORTANCE OF THE IRAQ INQUIRY

To return to this country. The British people used to trust the British State. This trust is the magnificent legacy of World War

Two, when we united in a common sacrifice to confront fascism.

Ever since then, we have regarded our state as ultimately decent and benign. We have understood that civil servants owed their loyalty to the state (symbolically expressed as the Monarch) rather than political parties or sectional interests.

It was also understood that there was a secret state which was unaccountable through normal democratic means. This was tolerated because we felt that British intelligence officers (in sharp contrast to their counterparts in many other countries) were decent, patriotic people.

This trust in the state was shattered by the Iraq War, and its gruesome aftermath. We have learnt that civil servants, spies, and politicians could not be trusted to act with integrity and decency and in the national interest. This discovery was shattering because it calls into question the moral basis on which Britain has been governed for the last hundred years or more.

This is why the Iraq Inquiry matters a great deal. It is the last chance for the British Establishment to show that it can learn the lessons of its failures – and hold those who fail to account. If Sir John Chilcot and his inquiry fail to achieve this, the Iraq Inquiry will be the final proof that our system of government is broken.